52 LITTLE LESSONS FROM
IT'S A WONDERFUL LIFE

OTHER BOOKS BY BOB WELCH

52 Little Lessons from A Christmas Carol

52 Little Lessons from Les Misérables

My Oregon

My Oregon II

My Oregon III

The Keyboard Kitten Gets Oregonized

The Keyboard Kitten: An Oregon Children's Story

Resolve

Cascade Summer: My Adventure on Oregon's Pacific Crest Trail

Easy Company Soldier

Pebble in the Water

My Seasons

American Nightingale

The Things That Matter Most

Stories from the Game of Life

Where Roots Grow Deep

A Father for All Seasons

More to Life Than Having It All

Bellevue and the New Eastside

52

LITTLE LESSONS

from

It's a Wonderful Life

BOB WELCH

NELSON
BOOKS

An Imprint of Thomas Nelson

52 Little Lessons from It's a Wonderful Life

© 2021 by Bob Welch

Published in Nashville, Tennessee, by Thomas Nelson. Thomas Nelson is a registered trademark of HarperCollins Christian Publishing, Inc.

Thomas Nelson titles may be purchased in bulk for educational, business, fund-raising, or sales promotional use. For information, please email SpecialMarkets@ThomasNelson.com.

Unless otherwise noted, Scripture quotations are taken from the Holy Bible, New International Version®, NIV®. Copyright © 1973, 1978, 1984, 2011 by Biblica, Inc.® Used by permission of Zondervan. All rights reserved worldwide. www.zondervan.com. The "NIV" and "New International Version" are trademarks registered in the United States Patent and Trademark Office by Biblica, Inc.®

Scripture quotations marked NKJV are taken from the New King James Version®. Copyright © 1982 by Thomas Nelson. Used by permission. All rights reserved.

Any internet addresses, phone numbers, or company or product information printed in this book are offered as a resource and are not intended in any way to be or to imply an endorsement by Thomas Nelson, nor does Thomas Nelson vouch for the existence, content, or services of these sites, phone numbers, companies, or products beyond the life of this book.

ISBN 978-0-7852-6570-2 (HC)
ISBN 978-1-4002-0394-9 (eBook)
ISBN 978-0-7852-6606-8 (Audiobook)

Library of Congress Cataloging-in-Publication Data

Welch, Bob, 1954-
52 little lessons from It's a wonderful life / Bob Welch.
    p. cm.
Includes bibliographical references (p.).
ISBN 978-1-4002-0393-2
1. It's a wonderful life (Motion picture) I. Title.
PN1997.I758W45 2012
791.43'7--dc23

2012010657

Printed in the United States of America

24 25 26 27 28 LBC 8 7 6 5 4

*To those with the conviction to believe
and those with the courage to explore.*

*The great need is not to do things,
but to believe things.*
—OSWALD CHAMBERS

Contents

Author's Note   xi

Lesson 1: God Honors Our "Childlike Faith"   1

Lesson 2: Underdogs Matter   7

Lesson 3: Sometimes You Just Gotta Dance   12

Lesson 4: You Matter to the World   16

Lesson 5: Self-Pity Skews Our Vision   20

Lesson 6: Life's Greatest Adventures Are
           About People, Not Places or Things   25

Lesson 7: You Can't Run Away from Your Problems   30

Lesson 8: It's Wise to Seek Counsel   35

Lesson 9: Stop to Count Your Blessings   40

Lesson 10: There's No Impact Without Contact   45

Lesson 11: When Criticized, Consider the Source   50

Lesson 12: Find Your Own Bedford Falls,
           Wherever You Live   55

Contents

Lesson 13: Trying to Keep Up with the Joneses Is Futile   58

Lesson 14: Perspective Changes Everything   63

Lesson 15: Prayer Changes Things   68

Lesson 16: Revel in the Accomplishments of Others   72

Lesson 17: Don't Wait to Tell Someone You Care   77

Lesson 18: Every Journey Has a Secret Destination   82

Lesson 19: Don't Look for What Is, but for What May Be   87

Lesson 20: It's in Helping Others That We Help Ourselves   92

Lesson 21: Life Is Not a Bed of Roses   97

Lesson 22: It Takes a Village to Raise a Child   102

Lesson 23: Quiet Lives Can Speak the Loudest   106

Lesson 24: No Man Is an Island   110

Lesson 25: God's Greatest Gift Is Life   114

Lesson 26: The Greatest Gift You Can Give Is Grace   118

Lesson 27: There's Much to Be Said for
Long-Term Commitments   124

Lesson 28: Actions Speak Louder Than Words   128

Lesson 29: Look for the Best in People   133

Lesson 30: Vengeance Is Not Ours, Saith the Lord   138

Lesson 31: Nobody Is Perfect . . . Which Brings Us to Grace   142

Lesson 32: The Essence of Life Is Relationships   147

Lesson 33: What Triggers True Change Is True Humility   151

Lesson 34: Fame Doesn't Equal Success,
Nor Obscurity Failure   157

Contents

Lesson 35: Bitterness Backfires on the One Who's Bitter   162

Lesson 36: Living Simply Helps Us
Appreciate What's Most Significant   166

Lesson 37: High Ideals Are an Honorable Pursuit   171

Lesson 38: Lost Dreams Can Be Found Opportunities   175

Lesson 39: All That Glitters Is Not Gold   179

Lesson 40: People Respond to Honorable Examples   183

Lesson 41: Helping Others Requires Sacrifice   186

Lesson 42: Look for Friends Who Bring Out the Best in You   191

Lesson 43: Desperation Can Be a Catalyst for Great Things   196

Lesson 44: Miracles Happen   199

Lesson 45: Age Is Insignificant; How You Live Is Not   203

Lesson 46: The Richest People in Town
Might Have Little Money   207

Lesson 47: The World Needs More Sentimental Hogwash   212

Lesson 48: Pay Attention to the Task at Hand   215

Lesson 49: People Can Change   218

Lesson 50: Entering a Child's World Expands Your World   223

Lesson 51: It Takes Time for Some Flowers to Bloom   226

Lesson 52: Life Revisions Strengthen the Script   230

Acknowledgments   235

Notes   237

About the Author   243

Author's Note

A bank in the city where I live has an interesting requirement for all new employees going through their orientation: they must watch a series of scenes from *It's a Wonderful Life*.

"The message in that film," the bank president told me, "is the message we want our employees to come to work with every day: the idea that our actions make a difference in the community around us."

I first watched the movie as a home-from-college kid in the mid-1970s. And over the decades I've come to appreciate the same thing that bank president appreciates about the movie. It is an hour-and-a-half-long "teachable moment."

From time to time over those years, I jotted down some of those lessons. Before long, I realized I had a lesson a week for a year: fifty-two bite-size nuggets of wisdom. Thus, the movie can be more than just holiday entertainment. Though our family, like so many others, has its traditional December viewing, it can inspire us to live better lives. To recognize what really matters. To be people of honor and integrity.

For nearly four decades, I've made my living writing books, magazine articles, and newspaper stories with a decided emphasis on people who inspire. George Bailey, Mary Hatch, and many of the rest of the *It's a Wonderful Life* cast certainly qualify as examples—and, in essence, they live on in all who take to heart the quiet but character-enriching lessons found in Bedford Falls.

—BOB WELCH
EUGENE, OREGON

LESSON 1

God Honors Our "Childlike Faith"

Yes, but he's got the faith of a child—simple.
—FRANKLIN THE ANGEL

It's a Wonderful Life's opening scene offers one of those blink-and-you-miss-it life lessons whose profundity might easily get lost. High in the heavens, the angels Joseph and Franklin, represented by two pulsing stars, are discussing who might be sent down to earth to deal with a suicidal man named George Bailey. Joseph suggests it's an angel named Clarence's turn, although, he laments, "He's got the I.Q. of a rabbit."

"Yes," says Franklin, "but he's got the faith of a child—simple."

This is high praise. Not only is it coming from an angel but apparently from a high-ranking angel, given that Franklin has the ultimate authority to make the call on who will be sent to earth in an attempt to save a man's life. Presumably, the angel pool stretches far beyond Joseph and Clarence. And yet Clarence is Franklin's "chosen one" in this case.

Why? It's certainly not because of his track record. Clarence is, after all, only an Angel Second Class. He hasn't earned his wings yet, and Franklin's comment that "We've passed him up right along" suggests it's not because he hasn't been given the chance to prove himself. Clarence himself suggests he has something of a sketchy record, telling Franklin he's been waiting for more than two hundred years to earn his wings, and "people are beginning to talk." Clearly, this is an angel with problems, not the least of which is an inferiority complex.

The idea that Clarence may not be the sharpest knife in the angel drawer is only underscored by his last name—Odbody—which not only suggests he is a tad quirky but may, in fact, come from a long line of quirky folks. Physically, he's underwhelming, sort of a Caspar Milquetoast in a seventeenth-century, embroidered nightshirt. And his ineptness is only bold-faced by Joseph's "I.Q.-of-a-rabbit" comment, assuming, of course, that Joseph's views aren't skewed by some sort of bias. And apparently they're not, given that Franklin doesn't disagree with Joseph on the matter. He seems to suggest that, yes, that may be true, but more important things are at work here.

Chief among those other things, Franklin suggests, is the angel's faith. And this is something so important that it trumps everything else.

So, exactly what is this "childlike faith" that Franklin holds in such high esteem? For starters, it's something not to be taken lightly. In Matthew 19:14, when the disciples rebuke those who have brought little children to Jesus, what does Jesus say? "Let the little children come to me, and do not hinder them, for the kingdom of heaven belongs to such as these."

Clearly, Jesus is big on children. He sees something special in them. He defends them in much the same way Franklin sees something in Clarence and defends him. But what is it about children's approach to faith that's so engaging? Though Jesus doesn't get specific about that, the answer is in their approach to life. As children, we are not jaded by the sophistication of the world. We're real. We're humble. We're willing to admit our needs and trust that others can help us. We're unpretentious and adventurous. We're lighthearted and imaginative. And we're fearless, willing to take a risk—a juvenile version of what the early twentieth-century Bible teacher Oswald Chambers calls "reckless joy."[1]

And then, of course, we grow up. And what happens? In many cases, we get jaded by the world. Instead of being real, we rationalize behaviors. We learn to put our personal spin on our shortcomings rather than deal with them. We become pretentious. We throw ourselves into all sorts of physical adventure but are cowardly regarding relationships, flitting from one person to the next, lacking the courage to commit.

We hide our needs from others. From God. From ourselves. We

play it safe, settling for too little in life. Rather than live by faith, we embrace one of many forms of legalism, be it a secular or religious version. Rather than try to please God with simple faith, we complicate things by trying to prove to Him how worthy we are by our works. We're full of fear, but we mask it with everything from busyness to addictions to rationalization, as we desperately seek to convince ourselves that we're content. In reality, we know little of Chambers's "reckless joy."

Not Clarence. No, sir. He's the real deal, living for some deeper ideals instead of simply going with the flow, ideals that stem from his childlike approach to life. Nick's Bar may be serving "hard drinks" for "men who want to get drunk fast," but Clarence orders the "mulled wine, heavy on the cinnamon and light on the cloves." He's unpretentious and honest. ("I didn't have time to get some stylish underwear. My wife gave me this on my last birthday. I passed away in it.") He's imaginative; remember, the point of insight on which the entire movie turns—George seeing what life would have been like without him—was Clarence's idea. And finally, he's a simple man—er—angel, full of childlike faith.

Clarence believes in George Bailey. He believes in his plan to help save him. But, above all, he believes in the One who sent him, and he exudes a certain sense of privilege that he's been chosen to be part of His plan.

Yes, he's a silly angel named Clarence. But director Frank Capra's use of him in this sense affirms deeper truths regarding a God who has often chosen the kind of people whom the larger world would not have: David, a lowly shepherd; Moses, a stutterer with low self-esteem; and Rahab, a prostitute. In choosing Clarence, Capra knowingly or unknowingly furthered a truth about childlike faith as suggested in 1 Corinthians 1:27: "But God chose the foolish things of the world to shame the wise; God chose the weak things of the world to shame the strong."

Given as much, might He also use imperfect people like you and me?

Read Matthew 19:14. How is Jesus "big on children," as the author says?

_____

_____

_____

_____

Clarence, Angel Second Class, has the simple faith of a child. Is your faith too complicated? What are some ways you could simplify your faith?

_____

_____

_____

Underdogs Matter

Just remember this, Mr. Potter, that this rabble you're
talking about . . . they do most of the working and
paying and living and dying in this community.
—George Bailey

It's 1928. Peter Bailey has died, board member Henry F. Potter wants to dissolve the Building and Loan, and Peter's son George, who is leaving for college, finds himself flying to the defense of his father's name.

Never mind that the taxi is waiting downstairs, presumably to take George to the train station where he's leaving for some engineering school to learn how to "build things." (And, please, dear reader, don't spend a nanosecond trying to figure out how Potter, in pre–Americans with Disabilities Act days, gets up to what appears to be the Building and Loan's second floor in that wheelchair of his.) The fact is, Peter Bailey's body isn't even cold yet, and grumpy old Potter is already smearing his rival's name.

Enter George, his black mourning band wrapped around the arm of his coat and his anger rising like Mount Saint Helens ash, circa 1980. Remember, this Potter-versus-Peter battle has been going on for at least a decade, since the day when a young George goes to his father for advice during the Mr. Gower-and-the-poison incident and hears Potter call his father a "miserable failure" who's not running a business but a "charity ward."

George stuck up for his father then—"He's not a failure!"—and sticks up for his father now. After Potter pooh-poohs Peter Bailey as a "starry-eyed dreamer" who squandered the business while trying to take care of the "lazy rabble" in town, George erupts.

"He didn't save enough money to send Harry to school, let alone me," he says. "But he did help a few people get out of your slums, Mr. Potter. And what's wrong with that?" Potter rolls his eyes and yawns. But George isn't finished. "Just remember this, Mr. Potter, that this rabble you're talking about . . . they do most of the working and paying and living and dying in this community. Well, is it too much to have them work and pay and live and die in a couple of decent rooms and a bath? Anyway, my father didn't think so."

The Baileys have long been—and, thanks to George, still are—champions of the underdogs, doers of Matthew 5:42: "Give to the one who asks you, and do not turn away from the one who wants to borrow from you." The Building and Loan is clearly a people place that gives down-and-outers the benefit of the doubt. The attitude isn't *Prove to me you deserve our help.* The attitude is *How can we help you help yourself?*

Potter turns down a loan application for Ernie Bishop, the cab driver who he says "sits around all day on his brains in his taxi." The Building and Loan gives him a five-thousand-dollar loan to help him and his family build a house.

Potter indirectly refers to Mr. Martini, owner of the Italian restaurant with a bar, as a "garlic-eater." Not only does the Building and Loan help Martini buy his own house but George and Mary spearhead the onsite celebration the day the family takes possession of it.

Admittedly, the movie depicts Violet Bick as a flirt who probably didn't do postgraduate work at MIT. (In the dance scene, you'll note she's the only girl dressed in black, a suggestion that she's a touch shady.) But if Potter sees her as a woman with loose morals and, when George comes to him on Christmas Eve, even suggests George and Violet are seeing each other on the sly, George treats her with great respect. At the dance, even when the sight of Mary causes George to pass up a dance with Vi, he has the decency to say, "Well, excuse me, Violet." More important, on that pivotal Christmas Eve, amid all the excitement of brother Harry having won the Congressional Medal of Honor and all the dread of the bank examiner wanting a look at the Building and Loan's books—and with George admitting to the bank examiner that the company is "broke"—he takes the time to see Violet when she stops by the office. Not only that, but we can presume the paper in the envelope he gives her is a written character reference for her move to New York. Then he hands her some of his own money to help her get started, implying, when she protests, that "It's a loan. That's my business. Building and Loan."

It's a subtly powerful scene: basically, one broke person giving another broke person a loan that we all know isn't a loan at all. It's an out-and-out gift. In Potter's world, he who dies with the most money and power wins; his commodity is power, and power equals virtue. But in the Baileys' world, he who has something—anything—should share with those who don't.

In the world's eyes—or at least old man Potter's—what matters is what you can get. In the Baileys', what matters is what you can give away. (Note that sign in Peter Bailey's office: "All you can take with you is that which you've given away."[1])

Who lives the richer life? Ask Mr. Potter on Christmas Eve when he sits alone in his office while the town raises a toast to George Bailey.

Who are some of the underdogs that Jesus encountered in His ministry? How was He a champion for them, and how did He minister to them?

_____

_____

_____

_____

Ultimately, old man Potter is very alone on Christmas Eve. How do greed and selfishness separate us from others?

_____

_____

_____

LESSON 3

Sometimes You Just Gotta Dance

You remember my kid sister, Mary?
Dance with her, will you?
—Marty Hatch

It's spring, and Mary Hatch and Harry Bailey are part of the 1928 graduating class that's holding its dance in the Bedford High gym— you know, the one with the retractable floor that unveils a swimming pool. (Filmed, by the way, at Beverly Hills High, where the gym-swim setup still exists.)

George, reluctantly, has shown up. Why? First, because Harry invited him during that high-energy dinner scene at the Bailey home earlier in the evening. "What do you mean," replies George, "and be bored to death?" And second, because his discussion with his father about possibly taking over the Bailey Building and Loan has cast the slightest ripple on his glass-smooth dream of going off to college and later, as he told his dad, to "build things . . . design new buildings . . . plan modern cities."

So even a high school dance—George is twenty-two in this scene—might take his mind off having perhaps disappointed his father or, heaven forbid, winding up "cooped up for the rest of [his] life in a shabby little office."

Never mind that Jimmy Stewart was thirty-eight when the movie was filmed; George is stuck in an awkward place: not really a man and not really a boy. He's not comfortable talking careers with Pops and not comfortable hanging with his brother's friends at the dance, a bunch of kids four years his junior.

To quote a sixties song, "then along comes Mary."[1]

Her older brother, Marty—he was in that opening sledding scene, riding his snow shovel down the icy hill just after George—asks for a favor. "You remember my kid sister, Mary? Dance with her, will you?"

George is the responsible type; "born older," his father says. Why would he want to dance with Marty's kid sister, that little girl at the soda fountain whom he first addresses as "brainless," that girl who—

Whoa! Suddenly, he sees her. *That's* why, he realizes as her soft-focus face looks his way. She's gorgeous. A flower now fully blossomed. (By the way, at that time Donna Reed was, at twenty-five, only seven years older than the Mary Hatch she played.) And yet, though George talks a good game—college, building modern cities, et cetera—you get the idea he's no risk-taker. After all, presumably, he's spent the last four years working for his dad at the Building and Loan. And he probably can't dance any better than old man Potter can smile.

But what does he do? He dances with Mary Hatch. And not some go-through-the-motions dance, but a spirited rendition of the Charleston, with broad-smile abandon, crisscrossing the knees with his hands and everything. He keeps dancing even after brother Harry announces this is a contest, which, of course, would have given him a nice excuse of "I'm not good enough." He keeps dancing even after the floor begins to part like the Red Sea. He even keeps dancing once he and Mary have fallen into the swimming pool.

And guess what?

It changes his life. Really. Had George not taken this small risk, he might never have wound up with Mary, who brings out the best in him, in their children, in Bedford Falls. Oh, and incidentally, there's a wisp of evidence later in the movie suggesting that George and Mary made a splash with the judges, too, and won that Charleston contest. In the bank run scene, while George stands at the window just prior to talking to old man Potter on the phone, you can see a trophy on a cabinet. It looks suspiciously like the one his brother, Harry, head of the dance contest, was holding up when announcing the event.

The safe route—comfort—is alluring, but it doesn't develop character. Or lead to possibilities. Or to winning dance contests. Or to falling in love and having one's life changed.

So, given the chance, dance. As George says, right after he tells Mary he's no dancer, "What can we lose?"

The gym dance is one of many joyful scenes in *It's a Wonderful Life*. What are some of the things that have brought you joy in your faith journey?

_____

_____

_____

_____

The author mentions that comfort, though alluring, doesn't develop character. What are some ways that God makes us uncomfortable so that we can grow?

_____

_____

_____

LESSON 4

You Matter to the World

*Strange, isn't it? Each man's life touches so
many other lives, and when he isn't around
he leaves an awful hole, doesn't he?*
—CLARENCE

On his Christmas Eve tour of "Life without George," our haunted hero has just had the door slammed in his face by his mother at Ma Bailey's boarding house. Not even she acknowledges knowing George, and how could she? After all, in Clarence's ploy to make George understand how much his life has mattered, he shows him life as if he had never been born.

After the encounter, the young Mr. Bailey is still convinced he's been placed under "some kind of spell" by Clarence, his desperation mirrored in one of those dramatic Capra close-up shots of George's face. It is a look of panic, of fear, of emotional discombobulation— quite the opposite of that upbeat close-up earlier in the movie, when Capra has his Wonder Boy freeze-frame while in pursuit of a suitcase so he can travel the world. ("I, I, I want a big one . . .")

Amid George's chaos, Clarence is leaning on the mailbox at the curb, holding his volume of *Tom Sawyer* in his hand. He then speaks the most profound line in the movie: "Strange, isn't it? Each man's life touches so many other lives, and when he isn't around he leaves an awful hole, doesn't he?"

In short, we matter. We make a difference. We are the proverbial pebbles in the water, our ripples going so much farther than we think.

Clarence knows the only way to restore George to wholeness is to make him understand this. So, with what we can assume are his God-given powers, Clarence decides to show George what life would have been like without him. Why? To remind him what life is like *with* him—the way his actions, words, and attitudes have affected those around him.

With George in the world, his brother, Harry, as a navy flier in World War II, saves an entire transport by shooting down fifteen planes, "two of them," Joseph reminds us, "as they were about to crash into a transport full of soldiers." Without George around to save Harry from falling in the ice in that opening scene, all those men died.

With George in the world, family, friends—heck, the community at large—are upbeat, productive, unselfish people. (A little far-fetched, sure, but plenty of inspiring movies stretch the bounds of credibility here and there, so what's a little schmaltz?)

With George in the world, Mr. Gower, the druggist, despite his understandable emotional lapse after the death of his son, is happy and sober; without George, he's a sad-hearted drunk who stumbles into Nick's Bar so lacking in esteem that he feigns acceptance in playing the part of the town fool.

Without George, Ernie the cab driver, instead of being the chatty chauffeur, is estranged from his "wife and kid"; George's mother is a sullen boarding house manager with a heart as cold as the river her son just plunged into; and Nick is a joyless bartender who runs a place designed to "serve hard drinks . . . for men who want to get drunk fast."

Clarence, it's clear, was right: we make a huge difference, and when we're not around, we leave terrible holes.

Without George having been around, Potter's power corrupts Bedford Falls—make that Pottersville. Violet, we can assume, has teetered over the line from the more innocent town flirt to a full-fledged prostitute. ("We'll wait for you, baby," the fellows tell her—and they probably don't mean for a game of Monopoly.) And Mary—well, librarians won't be thrilled to know that without George to marry her, she becomes, in Clarence's reluctant words, "an old maid" who "is about to close up the library." (As if had she become, say, an ax murderer who got married, things might not have been quite so bad.)

Forgive Capra's not-so-subtle sexism; he was a product of his times. And forgive his head-scratching decision to have a library still open until late on Christmas Eve. The bigger idea here is that in God's vast universe we matter, that our actions change the actions of others. And that when we're not around, we're missed.

In a world where it's easy to feel small and insignificant, could there be a more profound message in a movie?

The author calls this the most profound line in the film: "Each man's life touches so many other lives." Think of the people you love the most. What would your life be like without them, and theirs without you?

_____

_____

_____

_____

What are some of the ways you matter in God's vast universe?

_____

_____

_____

LESSON 5

Self-Pity Skews Our Vision

I wish I'd never been born.
—GEORGE BAILEY

The world is full of George Baileys: people who don't begin to under-stand how important they are to others. And often, they don't realize it for the same reason that George didn't realize it until his Christmas Eve adventures with Clarence: skewed vision.

Our significance to the world is skewed one direction if we think too highly of ourselves. Those with too much self-esteem tend to think the world would stop spinning if they weren't around; they tend to place too much importance on how much they influence those around them.

Our significance is skewed another direction if we think too lowly of ourselves. Never mind that those with too little self-esteem tend to be good-hearted people; they tend to think, like George, that if they've had any influence on others, it's usually been in a negative way.

In his Christmas Eve panic, George sees himself as the louse whose negligence is about to deep-six the business his father had begun; the mean-spirited husband who snaps at his wife; the frustrated father who berates his children; the community member who shouts down his daughter's schoolteacher and then rips into her husband when the man gets on the phone to defend her.

Me, make the world a better place? Right. In the scene inside the bridge's tollhouse, George scoffs at the idea when Clarence mentions it because his vision is too blurred by his self-pity. He may have started the day popping buttons with pride for his brother, Harry, the war hero, but he's ending it by letting his desperation blind him to a greater truth.

"No sin is worse than the sin of self-pity," wrote Oswald Chambers, "because it obliterates God and puts self-interest upon the throne. It opens our mouths to spit out murmurings and our lives become craving spiritual sponges."[1] There is nothing lovely or generous about that.

Self-pity is insidious and can strike without warning when we let circumstances cloud our vision. Consider that Christmas Eve in the movie. At the beginning of it, George couldn't be more upbeat. His brother, Harry, has won the Congressional Medal of Honor and is coming home for Christmas and a huge welcome from Bedford Falls. His mother has had lunch with the president's wife. All is well with the world. So cheerful is George that even the presence of a bank examiner doesn't faze him, even though he knows Bailey Building and Loan is running on empty.

Then Uncle Billy misplaces—or, more correctly, old man Potter steals—eight thousand dollars, and George's mood spirals from celebratory to suicidal in a matter of hours. The Bailey Building and Loan might have to close. Jobs will be lost. People will lose their money. And the honorable legacy of Peter Bailey, George's father, will be besmirched. As a frustrated George says to Uncle Billy, who hasn't a clue where the money went: "Do you realize what this means? It means bankruptcy and scandal, and prison!"

You can understand George sinking into the quicksand of despair, even if you realize that, until Clarence comes around, he's being victimized by his self-pity. Until this point in the movie, George has, for the most part, managed to stay emotionally afloat because of his connections with those around him. Mary, his family, his friends, and the community all give George a sense of purpose, even if at times he temporarily slinks into dissatisfaction or, in essence, has "his moments." Like when he turns down the offer to go to Florida with Sam and his girlfriend, then takes out his frustration by kicking his car door.

Alas, the desperation in his eyes as he stands on the bridge on this snowy Christmas Eve suggests more than temporary dissatisfaction. Why? Because in his self-pity George has cut off the very relationships that have sustained him: Mary, the children—and God, whom George sarcastically blames for "a bust in the jaw . . . in answer to a prayer."

And what brings him back to where he needs to be? A second-class angel who helps George see life with new eyes. Remember, what snaps George out of his self-pity is neither the money that saves the Building and Loan nor the people who bring it, though certainly he appreciates both. What snaps him out of it is not circumstances, but a new perspective he learns from his journey and affirms with his tearful "I-want-to-live-again" prayer on the bridge.

The snow begins to fall again, signifying that George has returned to real time and circumstances. But he is different from the man who stood on that bridge a few hours earlier, contemplating suicide.

Perspective changes our attitude. Changing our attitude breathes hope into us. And that's the real gift that God's messenger, Clarence, gives to George.

Hope. Like sunshine, it only breaks through to us when we remove the clouds of self-pity.

Which is worse: thinking too highly of yourself or too lowly? Or are they of equal detriment? Why or why not?

_____

_____

_____

_____

Have you ever thrown a pity party for yourself? How did you feel during it? Why do you think God does not want us to fall victim to our own self-pity?

_____

_____

_____

LESSON 6

Life's Greatest Adventures Are About People, Not Places or Things

Zuzu! Zuzu! My little gingersnap!
—GEORGE BAILEY

Even though this scene takes place in the middle of the worst depression in American history, George Bailey remains ever the would-be adventurer. As he and Uncle Billy await the arrival of George's brother, Harry, at the train station, he's lost in the wanderlust of going places and doing things. He tells Uncle Billy what the three most exciting sounds in the world are: "anchor chains, plane motors, and train whistles."

Four years have passed since George postponed his dreams of

going off to college by staying in Bedford Falls to keep the Bailey Building and Loan afloat after the death of his father. Now, Harry is returning from school; therefore, figures George, it's his brother's time to take over the family business while George finally spreads his wings and flies.

But the train scene changes everything. Harry, he realizes, hasn't arrived home alone. He's with his new wife, Ruth Dakin Bailey, whose father, it seems, has plans for Harry to work at his glass factory in Buffalo. "He wants to get Harry started in the research business," she tells George, beaming.

George's joyful expression morphs into panicked concern. Again, he realizes, his dreams will be thwarted. He'll be forever stuck in Bedford Falls, attached to Bailey Building and Loan as if it were a lead ball and he were the prisoner at the end of its chain.

Ah, but the movie's ultimate lesson is that for all the allure of going new places and doing exciting things, it's the people in our lives who really matter. And it's a lesson that George Bailey will, with the help of Clarence the Angel, ultimately learn—particularly when he finds his daughter Zuzu's petals in his pocket near the movie's end.

God loves people and, thus, so should we. He created people. He gave his Word to guide them. He forgives people. He, ultimately, gave His Son as a sacrifice for them. And yet how often do we live our lives as if what really matters is that research job in Buffalo? Or travel? Or adventure?

Not that there's anything wrong with going places and doing

things, with jobs and careers, with adventure. But to build our lives on such things is to place weight on that which cannot sustain us. How sad, it's been said, when we fall in love with things that cannot love us back.

"Do not store up for yourselves treasures on earth, where moth and vermin destroy, and where thieves break in and steal," said Jesus in Matthew 6:19. "But store up for yourselves treasures in heaven, where moth and vermin do not destroy, and where thieves do not break in and steal. For where your treasure is, there your heart will be also" (vv. 20–21).

The lesson is one not of geography but of priority. The suggestion isn't that we should all stay in our hometowns; George is correct in telling the ostensibly off-to-New-York Violet that "it takes a lot of character to leave your hometown and start all over again." Some people need to do exactly that: Join the military. Become a missionary. Take a job opportunity in a far-off city.

Instead, the suggestion is that wherever we go or whatever we do, we should make relationships our highest priority. When American sailor Robin Graham was sixteen, he embarked on a 33,000-mile, five-year trip around the world in a twenty-four-foot sailboat. What impressed me about Graham when I interviewed him years later in Seattle, Washington, wasn't only what he'd done. It was his realization that what he'd done—his grand adventure—wasn't enough to build a life on. After successfully reaching his goal, he moved to the wilds of Montana to build a log house, raise a family, and live off the land. By then, he was guided by deeper things, spiritual things, relational things.

Certainly, when he first considered the round-the-world voyage, his vision to see beyond the humdrum existence was admirable. "I loved the smell of rope and resin, even of diesel oil," he wrote. "I loved the sound of water slapping hulls, the whip of halyards against tall masts," he wrote in his first book, *Dove*. "These were the scents and sounds of liberty and life."

Thus did Graham ease out of San Pedro Harbor in Long Beach, California, on July 27, 1965, to conquer the world. Though you can argue against the practicality of such a voyage—I can't imagine giving a sixteen-year-old son of mine thumbs-up for such an adventure—you have to admire this about Robin Graham: he not only had the awareness of where he was but also had a vision for where he needed to go. How many people today live moored to regret because, instead of setting sail for some higher purpose, they've anchored themselves to the false security of affluence?

And Graham did it: sailed the world. But when it was over, he realized a certain hollowness to it all. What he longed for wasn't a deeper adventure, but deeper purpose, which he ultimately discovered when he found God. As Oswald Chambers wrote—not about Graham but about those who ground themselves in God's greater purpose: "He was at home with God wherever His body was placed."[1] In other words, life's deepest adventure isn't so much about places "out there," but about what's "in here"—our hearts. And we can live out those adventures regardless of where we sink our roots. "Remain in me," Jesus said in John 15:4, "and I will remain in you."

The bottom line: while the sound of "anchor chains, plane motors, and train whistles" may, indeed, tickle the imagination, George realizes that life abounds with deeper, more significant sounds, such as Zuzu running from her bedroom after hearing the voice of her father and crying, "Daddy!" Now *that's* an adventure.

George Bailey longs for adventure far away from Bedford Falls. What are the differences between worldly adventures and the adventure called faith?

_____

_____

_____

_____

Read Matthew 6:19–21. What do you think Jesus meant by "treasures in heaven"?

_____

_____

_____

LESSON 7

You Can't Run Away from Your Problems

Don't look now, but there's something funny going on over there at the bank, George. I've never really seen one, but that's got all the earmarks of a run.

—ERNIE THE CAB DRIVER

It is a day with more highs and lows than a volatile stock market: George and Mary's wedding day. For starters, it's raining (low). But who cares? Bedford Falls' most beloved couple is getting married (high). Ah, but trouble is brewing at the Bailey Building and Loan (low). The bank has called the business's loan, and Potter, conniving vulture that he is, has positioned himself to take full advantage, offering to pay fifty cents on the dollar if folks will move their money to his bank (another low).

But Mary saves the day when she offers Bailey customers the couple's honeymoon cash to tide them over until things settle down (high), then slips back to the old Granville house and, like a 1930s Martha Stewart, creates a cozy honeymoon suite, complete with a chicken roasting over the fire on a rotisserie driven by a phonograph player (triple high).

On a day full of lessons—we'll visit some of the others later in the book—among the most important is this: don't run away from your troubles. And the ink isn't even dry on their marriage certificate when George and Mary get their first taste of theirs.

Remember? They're being whisked off to their two-week honeymoon in the back of Ernie's cab, ostensibly headed for a train station. They're planning a week in New York and a week in Bermuda. "The highest hotels, the oldest champagne, the richest caviar, the hottest music, and the prettiest wife!" says George.

"That does it!" says Ernie. "Then what?"

"After that," says Mary, "who cares?"

You get the idea. George and Mary are, as the astute Ernie suggests, floating away "to Happy Land." And then, trouble. Ernie sees dozens of folks rushing beneath their umbrellas to Potter's bank and to Bailey Building and Loan. Director Frank Capra's use of rain and umbrellas is brilliant; after all, in a sense, the sky is falling. People are clamoring to withdraw whatever money they have in the Bailey Building and Loan.

George and Mary, the joy drained from their faces, stare out the back of the cab's window at a scene they can hardly believe. "Hey, Ernie," says a passerby, "if you got any money in the bank, you better hurry."

Mary mirrors the exact mindset that many of us would have in that moment, her brain quickly weighing two choices: leaving with the man of her dreams for a sunny, two-week honeymoon fueled by a sackful of wedding-gift cash, or staying to sort out a financial mess in rainy Bedford Falls. Many of us would say: "No brainer." In essence, so does Mary.

"George, let's not stop," she says. "Let's go!"

Who can blame her? She and George have been, for years, two ships passing in the night; now, fortune has changed. They're married. They're beginning a new life. They're enjoying arguably the happiest moments the two have ever shared, their life spread out before them in an ocean of possibilities.

Now this.

George, you can imagine, feels the same way she does. But in a quietly telling moment, he bases his decision not on feelings but on wisdom.

"I'll be back in a minute, Mary," he says, a statement that suggests naivete, sure, but courage as well.

What he's really saying is: *We've got to face this. We can't run away. Short-term pain for long-term gain.*

This is not a rap on Mary, who, by day's end, will twice be a hero. But it's George, in this case, who dares to see beyond himself to others, see beyond this moment to the long term, see beyond the fear that whispers, "Run, baby, run" to unlock his latent courage within. And look at the difference he makes. Given what transpires—again, more on that later—it's fair to say that George and Mary Bailey saved Bedford Falls that afternoon.

Let's consider for a moment what might have happened had they chosen to go instead of stay: An entire town goes "crawling to Potter." The people lose half of their savings while Potter fattens his pockets. The Bailey Building and Loan would likely have folded. True, George and Mary might have enjoyed a lavish honeymoon (if they could have overcome their guilt for abandoning the good people of Bedford Falls!). But would Mr. Martini have had the chance to "owna my own house"? No way. The Baileys' legacy of infusing Bedford Falls with heart and hope would have come to an abrupt halt. And Bedford Falls would forever be beholden to the "scurvy little spider" Mr. Potter if, in that decisive moment in the cab, George had said, "Yeah, you're right, Mary. The champagne is getting warm. To the train station, Ernie. Let's go."

Just like with George and Mary, sometimes we have a day marked by exhilarating highs and plummeting, discouraging lows that sometimes make us feel like running away. How does God's Word help you through days like these?

_____

_____

_____

_____

Life is full of choices. Think of a significant day in your life when you could have made a different choice. How might your life be different now?

_____

_____

_____

LESSON 8

It's Wise to Seek Counsel

Ask Dad, he knows
—Sweet Caporal sign in Gower's Drugs, noticed
by George as he's contemplating what to do about
the realization that Mr. Gower, in his grief, has
put poison in a pill bottle for him to deliver

Across Jefferson Avenue from Bailey Building and Loan, trouble is brewing at Mr. Gower's drugstore. Just after midnight on May 3, 1919, the town druggist received a telegram from the president of Hammerton College—yes, it's fictitious—saying Mr. Gower's son Robert has died of the flu. (Never mind that the influenza pandemic of 1918 had all but disappeared by then; it was far more realistic for that to be a cause of death in 1919 than now.)

By the time George shows up to work the soda fountain later that day, Mr. Gower has taken so much solace in a bottle that he's clearly drunk. Fumbling around with a bottle of pills, he drops some on the floor. He tells George to take the pills to a Mrs. Blaine, whose family has diphtheria, an ailment serious enough that, unchecked, it can lead to asphyxiation. Serious stuff, this. And yet the perceptive George notices something horrible about the powder Mr. Gower has apparently put in the capsules: it's poison!

"Mr. Gower," he says, "I think—"

"Aw, get going!" the druggist insists.

George isn't sure what to do. He's only twelve. He knows about poison. And he's being pressured to deliver it to a family. Should he obey Mr. Gower's orders or refuse those orders? Complicating his decision, of course, is that Mr. Gower is in no mood to discuss the issue—and, as an adult who is physically larger and George's boss, he clearly has a power advantage.

Glancing around, George sees the answer on a piece of advertising for Sweet Caporal cigarettes: "Ask Dad, *he* knows" the sign says. We're not sure what it is Dad is supposed to know—in 1919, based on the cigarette ad, it's clearly not the cancer-smoking link—but the look on George's face suggests that the proverbial lightbulb has gone off in his head.

In the next scene, George arrives at his father's workplace, the Bailey Building and Loan. He enters his father's office, only to find him going toe-to-toe with old man Potter over a five-thousand-dollar loan that Potter's bank wants repaid instantly. Peter Bailey pleads for a month's grace, which Potter, of course, dismisses like King Kong swatting a biplane atop the Empire State Building. The two get off on a tangent, initiated by Peter Bailey, about why Potter is, as Peter calls him, such a "hard-skulled character."

George interrupts, defends his father, and is politely ushered out by the man who, understandably, is engaged in an important business discussion. The camera shows George outside the door, the pills in his hand. What to do? What to do?

So, though he's seeking advice from his father, George doesn't actually get any. And, yes, you could argue that George, given the gravity of the situation, should have simply blurted out something like, "Dad, Mr. Gower wants me to deliver poison to someone!" But the scene infers that George is taking a WWDD approach to this dilemma: What Would Dad Do? And his subsequent return to the drugstore without having delivered the pills clearly suggests he knew what his father would have said: *No. Don't deliver the pills. Go back to Mr. Gower and explain the mistake that's been made.* Given his high character, we can also assume that the father, had he known what was at stake, would have taken George by the hand and gone with him across the street to Gower's.

George goes by himself. The druggist is angry that George hasn't carried out his orders. He slaps George so hard his ear starts bleeding, a young Mary Hatch—George's future wife—wincing with each blow as she sits at the soda counter in the front room. But Gower's anger quickly abates when George points out the error he's made. He then hugs a crying George, who, amazingly, amid this flurry of emotion, has the empathy to feel for the man and his loss, and the decency to say: "Mr. Gower, I won't ever tell anyone. I know what you're feeling. I won't ever tell a soul."

All of which is to say, George was wise in seeking advice from others. His pursuit of wisdom from his earthly father can be seen as symbolic of a believer's pursuit of wisdom from our heavenly Father. "Ask and it will be given to you; seek and you will find; knock and the door will be opened to you" (Matthew 7:7). Beyond what God's Word can offer us in terms of answers, we're told that seeking counsel from others—credible others—is a smart thing to do too.

George did exactly that. If there's a flaw in the God/Peter Bailey symbolic comparison, it's this: George's dad was too busy to listen to his son. But God is *never* too busy to listen to us. Says Matthew 28:20: "And surely I am with you always,"—*always*—"to the very end of the age."

Given as much, we should run to Him often—and with eagerness.

Read Matthew 7:7. What are some ways God opened the door to you when you sought His wisdom?

_____

_____

_____

_____

Like George approaching Mr. Gower, have you ever told the truth even when you were nervous or hesitant to do so? What happened? Was it worth it?

_____

_____

_____

LESSON 9

Stop to Count Your Blessings

Bread! That this house may never know hunger.
Salt! That life may always have flavor . . .
—MARY, AT THE DEDICATION OF THE
MARTINIS' NEW HOUSE IN BAILEY PARK

And wine! That joy and prosperity may reign forever.
—GEORGE, ADDING TO MARY'S BLESSING
ON THE MARTINIS' HOUSE

It's June 1934. Though the country is still deep in the Depression, George and Mary's intervention has saved Bedford Falls from the clutches of Potter. And, as if symbolic that a new day is dawning, the Martini family—Giuseppe, Marie, and four young children—are moving into their new home in Bailey Park, though you have to wonder if the new neighbors will be thrilled to see the Martinis' accompanying goats, rabbits, and turkey.

That said, this scene is about many things, not the least of which is hope. For years, the owner of Martini's restaurant, his wife, and his children have been stuck renting in the oppressive slums of a Potter "project," a cramped collection of little more than shacks. Now, at least one neighbor of Martini's, known in the script as "Mr. Schultz," thinks his neighbor is renting a house elsewhere. But Martini quickly corrects the man.

"I own the house. Me, Giuseppe Martini, I owna my own house. No more we live like pigs in thisa Potter's field."

Capra's 1971 autobiography, *The Name Above the Title*, suggests this scene was something of a microcosm of the life of Capra himself, who was born in Sicily and immigrated to the United States, where his family went on to live in a sort of Potter slum. "I hated being poor," he wrote. "Hated being a peasant. Hated being a scrounging newskid trapped in the sleazy Sicilian ghetto of Los Angeles . . . I wanted out."[1]

The new-house scene, if even unintentionally, also suggests a symbolic spiritual transformation that is not specific to Martini but applies to those who, like his family, are beneficiaries of grace. The slums-to-spanking-new-digs shift evokes 2 Corinthians 5:17: "Therefore, if anyone is in Christ, he is a new creation; the old has gone, the new has come!"

But beyond hope and transformation, this scene is mainly about celebrating the milestones of our lives. Though short and not packing the punch of other, more life-changing scenes, there's a sweetness to it spiced by Mary and George's dedication of the house. With the Martini family wrapped around them on the front porch, Mary holds up a baguette.

"Bread! That this house may never know hunger. . . ."

On the surface, Mary's opening line appears to be about physical sustenance: may you always have food to eat, clothes to wear, and a roof over your head. May your physical provisions always be taken care of. And yet it's interesting that Capra, a Catholic who clung to a quiet faith amid a sometimes-troubled life, chose bread as a symbol, similar to the way Jesus declares in John 6:35: "I am the bread of life. He who comes to me will never go hungry, and he who believes in me will never be thirsty." Whether Capra's real suggestion was related to building our lives on a God who promises us spiritual nourishment that's more sustainable than actual food, the choice of bread is intriguing, punctuated, as it were, by Maria crossing herself.

From bread Mary turns to salt. "Salt! That life may always have flavor." Again, interestingly, Capra chose a prominent biblical symbol, this one alluding to the verse in Matthew 5:13 regarding the way our lives can influence other lives: "You are the salt of the earth. But if the salt loses its saltiness, how can it be made salty again? It is no longer good for anything, except to be thrown out and trampled by men."

Finally, George concludes the couple's front-porch blessing by holding up a bottle. "And wine!" he says. "That joy and prosperity may reign forever." It is a symbol of celebration, something with which we can toast the goodness of life. At movie's end, in the Bailey living room, after George and Mary have emerged from their dark Christmas Eve with new hope, amid the revelry, Mary says, "Mr. Martini. How about some wine?" Again, another significant biblical symbol, beyond the admonition, of course, that we should be careful because it "bites like a snake" (Proverbs 23:32). Why? Because Jesus' first miracle involved turning water into wine at a wedding in Cana (John 2:1–11). And, in some ways, the Martinis going from renters with Potter to owners with the Baileys is a miracle.

In Michael Willian's *The Essential It's a Wonderful Life*, the author points out that Mary's blessing "is something of a cross between a Polish wedding tradition of presenting newlyweds with bread, salt, and wine, and a Russian housewarming tradition of bringing bread and salt to new home owners."[2]

The Martinis, of course, are not Polish or Russian but Italian. But given all the possibilities of why those three elements were chosen, perhaps the lesson is simply this: life's victories are worth celebrating.

The movie is replete with celebrations: Bedford Falls High's Class of 1928 graduation dance; at the Bailey home, Harry and Ruth's marriage, a party that was either originally intended as a welcome-home gathering for Harry or was a quickly-put-together celebration for the newly married couple at Uncle Billy's proclamation that "we're going to give the biggest party this town ever saw." There's also George and Mary's wedding, Christmas Eve at Martini's/Nick's, and, of course, the crowning scene: the redemption of George Bailey in the Bailey living room.

For now, perhaps it is enough that, through the help of others, a family who had little now has much. Not, of course, that the Martinis' little ranch house would be considered much in the jaded eyes of a Potter. But beauty is in the eye of the beholder, and clearly, the Martinis look up at their new abode as if it is some heavenly mansion. As Mary says: "Enter the Martini castle!"

It's a Wonderful Life is full of celebrations, including the one welcoming the Martinis to their new home. What are some of God's blessings that you can celebrate right now?

_____

_____

_____

_____

Read 2 Corinthians 5:17. How does knowing you are a new creation change your perspective?

_____

_____

_____

LESSON 10

There's No Impact Without Contact

*If you're going to help a man, you want to
know something about him, don't you?*
—JOSEPH

Ask casual viewers of the movie who Joseph was, and they probably wouldn't know. And why should they? He's never seen—and only mentioned a handful of times by name. But in the script, Joseph plays a significant role. He's one of the three heavenly voices we hear occasionally, the celestial stage managers, as it were, who set the original scene and help the transitions between other scenes.

Franklin is another one; he seems to be something of a supreme commander of angels, though he rarely speaks. And Clarence Odbody, Angel Second Class, is one, too, though of course he gets the call to descend from heaven and help instill hope in a man whom Franklin says is "thinking seriously of throwing away God's greatest gift"—his life.

Even if Joseph is destined to stay on the sidelines and offer commentary instead of being sent into the game like Clarence, he nevertheless offers some enlightening and emotional insight regarding the character of George Bailey; for example, there's that moving touch at the end of World War II: "Like everybody else, on V-E Day he wept and prayed . . ."

But one of his most significant lines is a nugget of wisdom he offers in the first scene, even if it is made with a bit of undies-in-a-bunch indignation. Joseph apparently had been on the prayer hotline and fielded the numerous calls for help from the folks of Bedford Falls regarding George Bailey. He goes to Franklin and with a sense of resignation suggests it's that "clock-maker's turn again." Clearly, Joseph is no fan of Clarence, the inference being that Odbody—as even his name suggests—is a loser angel who's not getting the job done on his missions. "He's got the I.Q. of a rabbit," Joseph chides. Nevertheless, Franklin makes the call: send down Clarence.

When Clarence arrives for his briefing, Joseph is less than polite. "Sit down," he says.

"Sit down?" asks Clarence, a bit discombobulated. "What are we—"

"If you're going to help a man, you want to know something about him, don't you?" says Joseph.

He says it with more than a touch of impatience; indeed, he

sounds downright angry, almost as if he and Clarence had had a falling-out centuries ago as earthlings, and Joseph still hasn't forgiven him. (Perhaps Clarence borrowed that copy of *Tom Sawyer* from Joseph and has yet to return it.) But all such context aside, Joseph has said something extremely important: before lending a hand to those in need, we need to know their stories. Context is important. Information is power. Why?

First, because it connotes respect for the person being helped, and every human soul deserves respect regardless of how different they are from us. God made us all.

Second, because it shows the person being helped that we're not just out for another notch on our belts. We're helping because we care. And part of caring is listening, understanding, empathizing, none of which can be done if we just barrel into a situation with all sorts of answers when we don't even understand the question.

Finally, because it will help us do our jobs better. When teaching interviewing skills to college students in journalism, I tell them the difference between a good exchange and a bad exchange is often the amount of homework you've done on your subjects. Why? Because it suggests you care enough about people's stories to learn something about them before engaging them in dialogue. In fact, I once brought a world-class marathoner in to class. "I can tell in the first few minutes whether interviewers have done their homework or not," he told the class. "If they have, I give them a deluxe interview. If they haven't, it's the basic burger."

Beneath that statement lies this truth: People respond to people they trust. And they trust people who care. So learning about someone is the first step in caring.

Why do most people attend a particular church? Because they know someone in that church; they've had contact with someone whose life has had an impact on them. That's easy if it's someone just like us. But what about the people we meet who are far different from us? We tend to shy away, fearing a chink in our comfort armor, instead of getting to know them.

When Jesus met the Samaritan woman at the well, He knew the context far beyond the fact that, as a Jew, He wasn't expected to be mixing it up with a Samaritan. "You are right when you say you have no husband," He said. "The fact is, you have had five husbands, and the man you now have is not your husband" (John 4:17–18). He knew her story. And knowing her story enabled Him to appreciate her need for "living water" (see verse 13).

Missionaries don't lumber into villages and say, "See it our way or else." They learn the people's stories. Counselors don't simply spew out advice; they get to know their clients. And likewise, angels portrayed in *It's a Wonderful Life* can't expect to help someone without knowing him.

Clarence heeds Joseph's advice. In the hour he has before heading to earth, he learns about George. Hears his story. Learns what he will later tell George after the two have been thrown out of Nick's Bar: "You have no papers, no cards, no driver's license, no 4-F card, no insurance policy"—the things that, ultimately, convince George that Clarence is the real deal and genuinely cares about him. And earns him enough trust to allow him to lead George back home.

Interacting with someone we know nothing about can take us out of our comfort zone. Why do you think God wants us to reach out to and care for others unlike ourselves?

_____

_____

_____

_____

Think of acquaintances in your life that you wish you knew better. What are some ways you can show God's love for them?

_____

_____

_____

When Criticized, Consider the Source

*So, I suppose I should give [the money] to
miserable failures like you and that idiot
brother of yours to spend for me.*
—MR. POTTER

Henry F. Potter may be the richest man in town at movie's start, but his bedside manner is pathetic. Consider the bile he flings around about people: he calls Peter Bailey a "miserable failure" to his face and, in the same breath, refers to Peter's brother, Uncle Billy, as an "idiot."

After Peter dies, Potter may ratchet down his verbal scorn a touch, but he's still mean-spirited, dissing Peter Bailey's "high ideals" as unaccompanied by any "common sense" and thus, apt to "ruin this town." He derides cab driver Ernie Bishop as a guy who "sits around on his brains all day." In the scene where he tries to hire George, Potter refers to the people the Baileys try to help as "a lot of garlic-eaters," a racial slur aimed at Italians such as the Martinis. And in the final scene in which he appears, Potter calls George "a miserable little clerk crawling in here on your hands and knees and begging for help." His final act is to seek a warrant for George's arrest.

But in the end, it's George being honored as "the richest man in town," the Baileys' living room being packed with people who know, love, and respect him—not Potter. Which reminds us of an important truth: the opinions about us that count are the opinions of the people we respect, not the ones we don't.

When people criticize us, particularly with the bile of resentment, it says less about us than about them. In some cases, it says they want what we have. It evokes jealousy. Insecurity. Smallness. Of course, Potter despises the Baileys: in their bumbling, substance-over-style ways, they represent everything he knows, deep down, he's called to be and nothing that he is. He resents that, despite living on the financial edge, they seem to have found a certain peace, contentment, and purpose. And it galls him that despite his enormous wealth, he has found none of the three. As Peter Bailey astutely observes, Potter "hates everybody that has anything that he can't have."

When we realize our shortcomings, our character always determines *which of two paths* we'll take. We can either (1) humble ourselves and, with a willingness to change, aspire to be more or (2) puff up with pride and, unwilling to change, rationalize our stubbornness. In the latter case, the leverage that moves our egos upward is the same force that pushes those we secretly envy downward. For Potter, to give any credit to the Baileys would be to discredit himself, because he knows he is the polar opposite of them.

The Baileys care about others. Potter cares only about himself. "He's a sick man," Peter Bailey tells George in what, we'll soon learn, is his last conversation with his son. "Frustrated and sick. Sick in his mind, sick in his soul, if he has one."

If this is true—and, clearly, it is—why would anyone allow himself to be defined by someone with such a skewed outlook on life?

In my early years as a newspaper columnist, I found myself often being wounded by barbed responses to my articles. That, of course, is the nature of the business: you traipse out an opinion, and others are free to criticize it. But a sage former journalism professor of mine offered three words that have spared me all sorts of pain: "Consider the source." Take seriously the criticism from people whose lives bring credibility to their views on life; ignore the rest.

Over the years, I've taken that to heart. At times, I've received criticism from people I know and respect. Sometimes I've found myself agreeing that they make a good point. Perhaps I overlooked something about a situation. Perhaps my point of view resulted from skewed vision. Perhaps I had some bias I hadn't recognized and it caused me to take a stance on an issue or person that, after further review, I realize wasn't justified. In other words, I came to a fork in the road and realized that I needed to humble myself and change, in this case, a viewpoint.

More often, I've realized that people who criticized me weren't so much targeting me as venting a frustration embedded deep in their own lives. It's the kind of frustration that plagued Potter, even if he worked hard to avoid facing it—the kind of frustration George described when he said to Potter: "I know very well what you're talking about. You're talking about something you can't get your fingers on, and it's galling you."

Criticism happens. We can't avoid it. But like the Baileys, we would do well to consider the source, refuse to be defined by someone else, and as Romans 12:21 says, "overcome evil with good."

Have you ever been on the receiving end of a hard truth? How did God use it for good?

_____

_____

_____

_____

Mr. Potter is deeply unhappy and seems devoid of humility. Why is humility so important in our walk with God?

_____

_____

_____

Find Your Own Bedford Falls, Wherever You Live

Homesick? For Bedford Falls?
—George to Mary

Yes.
—Mary

Every so often, some critic will take a shot at *It's a Wonderful Life*, specifically at director Frank Capra's depiction of Bedford Falls as a sort of Norman Rockwell town. "All hail Pottersville!" said a piece on Salon.com in 2001. "Pottersville rocks!" But Bedford Falls? It is, the article says, "the kind of claustrophobic, undersized burg where everybody knows where you're going and what you're doing at all times."[1]

In the life-without-George sequence, Bedford Falls becomes a darker, more hard-edged place where the emphasis is on booze, women, pounding music—you get the idea. But those who miss the virtues of Bedford Falls are apparently those who miss the virtues of human connections that extend beyond the proverbial one-night stand.

It's almost irrelevant what show is playing at the town movie theater or what music is being played in Bedford Falls' local bars. Its charm lies in its people. In the community connectedness. In people feeling part of something.

In Bedford Falls, there's a shared history. A shared pride. A shared concern about not only the place but also the people in that place.

The point isn't that we should all move to small towns. The point is that we're fortunate if, wherever we live, we can carve out lives in those places where "people are a priority." Where we're accountable to others. Where we understand that the actions of a few affect the larger community.

That may be in the form of a church, a small group, a neighborhood, a family, a club, a school, but they are organizations in which people draw together for a common cause. The critic panned Bedford Falls, in part, because everybody knows what everybody else is up to. But, to some degree, isn't that also the kind of built-in accountability that makes us want to live to a higher standard—because we realize we'll be letting someone down if we don't? That our actions matter to the whole? And isn't that what enabled Mary to rally much of the town to help George?

Frankly, that "high-touch" dimension has gone missing in America in the last fifty years. Bedford Falls reminds us that if it's impractical for us to all live in small towns, we should seek ways to find that "small-town community" wherever we live. For like logs on a fire, we burn brightest when huddled together with others.

The author writes that "we burn brightest when huddled together with others." Thinking of your own group or community, what are ways that you shine brightly to the world?

_____

_____

_____

_____

Look up the definition of "accountability." How is accountability manifested in our faith journey?

_____

_____

_____

LESSON 13

Trying to Keep Up with the Joneses Is Futile

Daddy, the Browns next door have
a new car. You should see it.
—PETE BAILEY

Few would argue with the premise that George Bailey is among the more well-grounded individuals around. And yet like us all, George has his temptations—and well beyond the scene in which Violet Bick crosses the street in that fanciful dress, causing George's jaw to drop and his mouth to exclaim, "Hey, you look good. That's some dress you got on there." To which she responds with that great line, "Oh, this old thing? Why, I only wear it when I don't care how I look."

A more insidious tug on George's conscience is his occasional temptation to bag what he sometimes sees as a humdrum life and keep pace with others in the sense of material possessions. To, in essence, "keep up with the Joneses." (Though never used in the movie, the term came of age about the time George Bailey was coming of age; the phrase was popularized when a comic strip of the same name was begun by Arthur R. "Pop" Momand in 1913.)

George's frustration with keeping pace with others manifests itself a number of times in the movie, foremost among them, when after helping dedicate the new Martini home in Bailey Park, George and Mary are asked by Sam Wainwright to join him and his wife in Florida. Sam is a longtime friend of George's; that's him hee-hawing in the sledding scene when we first meet a young George Bailey. But the two are as different as salt and pepper. After the pivotal phone scene in which Sam encourages Mary and George to get in "on the ground floor" of a factory his dad is going to start to make plastics out of soybeans, George turns to Mary, knotted in frustration: "Now you listen to me! I don't want any plastics! I don't want any ground floors." In other words: *Listen to me! I don't want to be Sam Wainwright.*

Ah, but deep down, in some ways, George *does* want to be Sam Wainwright. Sam's presence bothers George because Sam left Bedford Falls and is doing all the "important things" that have eluded George. That's clear from the scene in which George and Mary are offering the bread, salt, and wine to the Martinis, and George notices Sam and his new wife in the street, standing beside their chauffeur-driven town car. George is mildly irked by his friend's presence. ("Sam Wainwright!" he says to Mary while nodding toward the street, to which Mary replies: "Oh, who cares," her barbed response suggesting that she knows George struggles with Sam.)

Sam is living the life of luxury while George is "fighting the battle of Bedford Falls." Remember, too, that Sam, if even from afar, once had his eye on Mary. Much to the delight of Mary's mother, Sam called her the night George stopped by after wandering away from the party honoring newlyweds Harry and Ruth. And though George never comes across as an "I-need-the-credit" sort of guy, it was George who'd given Sam this plastics-from-soybeans idea—an idea that, by the way, Henry Ford was in fact implementing at the time. (Sam: "Remember that night in Martini's Bar when . . . you told me you read someplace about making plastics out of soybeans? Well, listen. Dad snapped up the idea.") So, Sam's father hands his son a soy-based golden goose, and George's father hands his son a struggling building and loan business. What's more, it was George who suggested that Sam anchor a factory to produce that plastic in Bedford Falls, an idea that Mr. Wainwright subsequently implements. Outside the Martinis' new house, Sam says, "We just stopped in town to take a look at the new factory, and then we're going to drive down to Florida."

When he invites George and Mary to join them, the divide between the two men has never been wider, at least from George's perspective. He has neither the time nor the money for such a whimsical foray. As Sam and his wife whisk themselves off to sunny Florida, Wainwright's trademark "hee-haw" grates on George like fingernails on a chalkboard. In that moment, George is tired of keeping his nose to the old grindstone. He'd rather be carefree Sam Wainwright. As he kicks closed the door on his non–chauffeur-driven car, his frustration erupts.

In the subsequent scene, Potter offers George a job. The juxtaposition of the no-to-Florida scene and yes-to-Potter scene, at least initially, is brilliant on Capra's part. Here's George Bailey, who, in one scene, laments that he doesn't have more—that he can't whisk his wife off to Florida for a vacation—and in the next scene, is offered just that: more. Way more. A chance to become exactly what he's lamenting he's not. "You wouldn't mind living in the nicest house in town . . . You wouldn't mind that, would you, George?" teases Potter.

A final example: in George's Christmas Eve meltdown, son Pete inadvertently adds fuel to his father's fire of frustration by announcing that the neighbors have a new car. "Well, what's the matter with our car?" George snaps. "Isn't it good enough for you?" (Read, "What am I—a failure because I'm not Mr. Brown or Sam Wainwright, because I essentially became my father, because I never went off to build things, design new buildings, and plan modern cities?")

But Clarence the Angel changes everything. George's trip back to never-been-born land, if painful for him in places, washes away all that insidious craving for what others have. And it reminds him that he has all that he needs.

It's a Wonderful Life offers subtle messages about materialism, a theme that also comes up often around Christmastime. Why is having more not necessarily a spiritually healthy aspiration?

_____

_____

_____

_____

Sam Wainwright's success is George's constant reminder of "what could have been." What are the things in your life that give you contentment and are more meaningful than the things you possess?

_____

_____

_____

LESSON 14

Perspective Changes Everything

Oh, look at this wonderful old
drafty house. Mary! Mary!
—George Bailey

What is different about George Bailey's life after Clarence shows him what life would have been like without him? When he realizes, on that snowy bridge, that Zuzu's petals are back in his pocket? When he's running down the streets of Bedford Falls, wishing everybody, including the Building and Loan, a "Merry Christmas!"?

In terms of circumstances, absolutely nothing.

Remember, at this point, for all he knows his life is exactly as it was a few hours before; Clarence did nothing to change that. To wit: Bailey Building and Loan has still lost eight thousand dollars and, with the bank examiner in town, is in serious danger of failing. George and his extended family members—beyond Uncle Billy, Cousin Eustace, and Cousin Tilly—will be out of jobs, and the money of hundreds of people who've trusted in the Building and Loan may be lost. Worse, George can assume from Potter's threat that there is a warrant out for his arrest. A reporter from the *Bedford Falls Sentinel* is likely at work on a story that has embezzlement written all over it; after all, how does one just suddenly lose eight grand?

All these pitfalls almost make the more minor things George complained about hours earlier seem trivial: the "drafty old barn" that George and his family "have" to live in. (Darn that staircase newel anyway!) The struggles of a large family. ("You call this a happy family? Why did we have to have all these kids?") The fact that the Browns have a new car and the Baileys do not. Finally, of course, there's that little spot fire regarding Zuzu's teacher, on which George, in his anger, poured gasoline when he verbally ripped her on the phone and then threatened her husband, who'd come to her defense.

Given this tangled web of woe, perhaps George summed it up best back in his Christmas Eve tirade after Mary asked him what was wrong: "Wrong? Everything's wrong!"

And, again, nothing about these circumstances has changed a bit as George races home after his interaction with Clarence. So, why is he wishing the whole community—heck, even Mr. Potter —a "Merry Christmas!"? Why, when he comes into his house, is he smiling, laughing, shaking hands with the bank examiner, and extending season's greetings to the sheriff, who's handing him a warrant for his arrest? Smiling for the *Sentinel*'s photographer? Kissing that detachable newel post in what's now a "wonderful old drafty house"? Gathering his children in his arms? Hugging Mary as if he'd just returned from war?

Indeed, if the circumstances of George's life are, as far as he knows, unchanged at this point, why is he brimming with life and enthusiasm and love?

Because *he's* changed, that's why. His attitude. His perspective. Thus, even though there's a colossal mess to be untangled, he really doesn't care a fig. Because the stuff that *does* matter—family, friends, and faith—has now risen to such preeminence in his life that the rest doesn't really matter. He has a sort of blind faith that whatever he has to get through, he can get through because he sees clearly now. The scales have fallen off his eyes. He realizes, even before brother Harry swoops in to remind everybody, that he is, indeed, the richest man in town.

Pastor Charles Swindoll of Dallas, Texas, said it so well:

The longer I live, the more I realize the impact of attitude on life. Attitude, to me, is more important than facts. It is more important than the past, than education, than money, than circumstances, than failures, than successes, than what other people think or say or do. It is more important than appearance, giftedness or skill. It will make or break a company . . . a church . . . a home. The remarkable thing is we have a choice every day regarding the atti-tude we will embrace for that day. We cannot change our past . . . we cannot change the fact that people will act in a certain way. We cannot change the inevitable. The only thing we can do is play on the one string we have, and that is our attitude . . . I am convinced that life is 10% what happens to me and 90% how I react to it.

It's easy to forget that in *It's a Wonderful Life*, the real change that George undergoes has nothing to do with that laundry basket full of money, nor, really, with the affection his friends shower on him on that Christmas Eve. That's just the circumstantial frosting on the new-attitude cake. The real change is within his soul. For the first time, George Bailey looks at life with new eyes.

Perspective Changes Everything

We all struggle with our attitudes. How does a good attitude affect your family, friends, and faith? What about a bad attitude?

_____

_____

_____

_____

One of the highlights of the film is George's rapturous change of heart. Has something ever brought about such a change of heart in your own life?

_____

_____

_____

LESSON 15

Prayer Changes Things

I'm the answer to your prayer. That's
why I was sent down here.
—Clarence the Angel, after George tells him
"I got a bust in the jaw in answer to a prayer"

When George Bailey sidles up to Martini's Bar on Christmas Eve, he's at the lowest point of his life. In the span of only a few hours, he has: (a) learned that the Bailey Building and Loan has lost eight thousand dollars just as the state's bank examiner shows up; (b) all but threatened to kill Uncle Billy, who has apparently lost the money; (c) estranged himself from the people he loves most, Mary and the kids; (d) heard from old man Potter that a warrant is out for his arrest; and (e) had his desperate plea for a loan turned down by Potter, the man with whom his family has struggled for decades.

Against that backdrop, he's had enough drinks to cause Martini's assistant, Nick, to soon ask if he wants a ride home. An obviously concerned Martini will ask why George is drinking so much and encourage him to go home and spend Christmas Eve with his family.

But first, George does something he admits he does not want to do: he prays. "Dear Father in Heaven," he begins. "I'm not a praying man, but if you're up there, and you can hear me, show me the way. I'm at the end of my rope. I . . . Show me the way, God." Whereupon a man next to him at the bar, a Mr. Welch (no relation), learns that he is George Bailey and proceeds to coldcock him with a right jab in defense of his wife the schoolteacher, whom George had berated on the phone. As he composes himself after the knockdown, George mutters, "That's what I get for praying."

No, what he gets for praying is Clarence—and a new lease on life. In the movie's opening scene, the angels Franklin and Joseph are hearing the prayers of townspeople—Mr. Gower, Martini, and Ernie—and family members: George's mother, Mary, Janie, and Zuzu.

"A lot of people are asking for help for a man named George Bailey," says Joseph. But it's clear that the angels have heard the prayers of George, too, and know his muddled mindset. Franklin knows, for example, that George will be standing on that snow-swept bridge at 10:45 P.M. and "thinking seriously of throwing away God's greatest gift"—"Oh, dear, dear! His life!" chimes in Clarence. He couldn't have known that based only on the prayers of the others. And in George and Clarence's first conversation, as they dry out in the bridge tollhouse, the angel is up front about why he's come.

"Your lip's bleeding, George."

"Yeah, I got a bust in the jaw in answer to a prayer a little bit ago."

"Oh, no, no, no, George, *I'm* the answer to your prayer," says Clarence. "That's why I was sent down here."

Not that George buys into that without some very serious proof on the part of Clarence; he has the doubt gene of the disciple Thomas. But after George is shown life without him having lived it, after nobody recognizes him, after Mary runs away from him and Bert the cop fires shots toward him—he comes to his second moment of desperation, the first, of course, being the bar scene. And what does he do?

He prays again. "Clarence! Clarence! Help me, Clarence. Get me back. Get me back. I don't care what happens to me. Only get me back to my wife and kids. Help me, Clarence, please! Please! I want to live again. I want to live again. I want to live again. Please, God, let me live again."

And what happens when he utters God's name? The snow begins to fall. Zuzu's petals return to his pocket. And hope returns to the soul of a man who, only a short time earlier, was prepared to commit suicide. That, not the punch from the schoolteacher's husband, is George's answer to prayer: the will to live again.

We've all been on that bridge of despair at some point in our lives. The answer isn't looking down at the waters below, but looking up at the heavens above.

Doubt often goes hand in hand with faith. What are some things you are doubting right now that need to be given to the Lord in prayer?

_____

_____

_____

_____

Think of a time in your life when you were on the edge of despair. How did prayer help give you the strength to "live again"? Read Romans 8:35–39 as an encouragement.

_____

_____

_____

LESSON 16

Revel in the Accomplishments of Others

*Very jealous. Very jealous. He only
lost three buttons on his vest.*
—Billy to Henry Potter regarding George's
reaction to news of Harry winning the
Congressional Medal of Honor

George Bailey is nothing if not human. He longs for things he does not have. He is envious, in some ways, of Sam Wainwright. He gets angry, even at his own family. But he is chock-full of virtues too; among them is his willingness to help others without requiring pats on the back for his goodness. That's called humility.

Think about it: When does George ever gloat over his success? He saves the life of his brother, Harry, who's struggling in that icy pond, but where were the headlines in the *Bedford Falls Sentinel*? After his father's death, when he gives up his college dreams to run the Building and Loan, nobody declares "George Bailey Day." Along with Mary, he helps save the Bailey Building and Loan on their rainy wedding day but receives no praise for the act. He quietly gives money to Violet Bick to help her get a new start in New York, but, beyond a kiss on the cheek from her, nobody's promoting George as Humanitarian of the Year.

In fact, Potter uses that good deed against him, suggesting, during George's Christmas Eve plea for a loan, that the gesture might signal trouble at home for George. (Nitpickers, of course, might wonder how word of that loan got out to anyone in the first place, much less to Potter in only hours. It happened, after all, behind closed doors. And, true, Cousin Tilly, Cousin Eustace, and the bank examiner witness George's peck on the cheek from Vi, but are we to assume one of them—or Vi herself—spread the word?)

Oh, people are thankful for George and his concern for others. Vi is clearly appreciative of his generosity. So is Mr. Gower, who bought George a special suitcase as the young man readied for his planned trip around the world, undoubtedly still remembering the incident when George, as a boy, saved the druggist's hide by not delivering the poison pills. But nobody's singing George's praises to the public at large. Neither, significantly, is George asking for any such thanks.

In essence, George Bailey is the embodiment of Matthew 6: "Be careful not to do your 'acts of righteousness' before men, to be seen by them. If you do, you will have no reward from your Father in heaven. So when you give to the needy, do not announce it with trumpets, as the hypocrites do in the synagogues and on the streets, to be honored by men" (vv. 1–2).

George does the right thing because it's the right thing, not because it'll earn him strokes with people around him. He's a virtue-is-its-own-reward kind of guy. He invests in people in quiet, behind-the-scenes ways that keep the focus not on the giver but on the one being given to.

Take the scene in which the Martinis move into their new home. The focus is on the Martinis, not on the Bailey Building and Loan, which made this dream possible. Yes, that's George Bailey trying to herd a goat and the Martini kids into the car. In our current times, when public relations folks spin good deeds into "look-what-we-did" Web announcements and tweets, the only reason the head of a lending company would stoop to such a level would be to capitalize on a good photo op.

But George not only doesn't need the spotlight; he's happy to shine it on others. When Harry wins the Medal of Honor, George passes out copies of the newspaper with his brother's story on the front. Potter, always looking for the evil in others to justify the evil in himself, suggests to Uncle Billy that the news must be making George, who was turned down by the draft board because of his bad ear, feel jealous, overshadowed.

"Very jealous. Very jealous," says Uncle Billy. "He only lost three buttons on his vest."

Despite his concern about what brother Harry's marriage plans might do to his future—remember the train-station scene in which wide-eyed George freezes at Harry's words, "Meet the wife"?— George doesn't slink into self-pity. (Well, okay, later, when he leaves the party for a walk, he might at least be testing the self-pity waters.) Though he's been emotionally jolted, he recovers as if to say, *What's important here isn't me, but Harry and Ruth.* "What am I doing?" George stammers, then kisses his new sister-in-law on the cheek, disarming his inner turmoil with humor: "What's a pretty girl like you doing marrying this two-headed brother of mine?"

George's willingness to honor others above himself, of course, spirals to an ironic twist at movie's end: a lifetime of giving culminates in all the people to whom he's given lavishing praise, money, and honor on him in return. As such, the movie's final scene brings to mind a passage in Matthew 6 that suggests that if nobody else sees our good deeds, God does. "Do not let your left hand know what your right hand is doing, so that your giving may be in secret. Then your Father, who sees what is done in secret, will reward you" (vv. 3–4).

Acts of goodness and grace are often better done out of the public eye. What are some ways you can make a difference in someone else's life behind the scenes?

_____

_____

_____

_____

George Bailey's concern and respect for others is a persistent theme throughout the film. List three ways Jesus showed this same virtue in Scripture.

_____

_____

_____

LESSON 17

Don't Wait to Tell Someone You Care

Pop, you want a shock? I think you're a great guy.
—George, to his father at dinner

It's the night of Harry's graduation dance, and while the young man is upstairs getting ready, George and his father, Peter, chat while finishing up their meals. Pop asks son George if he has any interest in taking over Bailey Building and Loan. George makes it clear that he'd rather do other things. Then, out of the blue, he says it: "Pop, you want a shock? I think you're a great guy."

Only hours later, Peter Bailey will be dead. But what child wouldn't want his or her last words to a parent to be something like what George told his father—that, in so many words, he loved him? And what parent wouldn't simply glow inside after hearing such an affirmation, regardless of whether that mom or dad died that night or decades later?

Outwardly, George's words get lost in the light banter between Annie, the family's maid, and George, who invites her to pull up a chair. And, sure, Peter Bailey is disappointed that George so easily brushes off the idea of taking over the family business. That said, you have to believe it was reassuring for Peter Bailey to know that his son respected him so much.

Assuming people care about us isn't the same as actually being reminded that they care; indeed, words, gestures, or, in this case, an entire event speak volumes. As I write this, I've just returned from just such an event. In what became our community's version of the movie *Mr. Holland's Opus*, an eighty-five-year-old former high school choir director led his students—now in their forties and fifties—in a ten-song concert at their old high school. At their request. (In *Opus*, a sixty-year-old retiring band director played by Richard Dreyfuss is surprised in the auditorium by his former students, who hand him a baton and, to honor him, play the opus that he had written but never heard played.)

In the real-life event I attended, classes from 1969 to 1982 that had sung under the same man gathered to honor their director and mentor. The auditorium was packed. The atmosphere was magical. The bond between director and students was obvious. We all walked out of the event as if floating on air, so inspiring was this blend of music, time, respect, honor, and things even deeper.

In fact, during the program, the director told the audience this really wasn't about music. "What this is really about is love. I love them and, for some reason, they love me."

In a dog-eat-dog world, where the daily news is so often about just the opposite of love, this decades-old story was a privilege to be part of. But why did it happen in the first place? Because people saw the importance of communicating to the man how they felt. And they went to the trouble of doing so in an amazingly special way.

The event was a year in planning. Former students with busy lives returned to their high school town from across the country. That took money. Time. Effort. Preparation. It took all sorts of sacrificing.

I happened to be at a restaurant after the Saturday night finale when the honoree walked in to join his family, who had come to Oregon from as far away as Florida for the event. A smattering of clapping began. Then, much of the restaurant, knowing the story, also began applauding the man. A moment to behold.

We only have so much time to tell the people we love that we love them. In most cases, it can be done far easier, quicker, and cheaper than this event: A word. A letter. An email. An out-of-the-blue present or surprise trip. The "how" is the insignificant part. What's important is not waiting until it's too late.

Once, while leading a men's retreat, I passed out small packs of sticky notes. Whenever I mention the idea of telling someone you love how you feel, I'll inevitably hear the comment "You're a writer. It's easy for you to do. It's much harder for the rest of us." I heard it again at this retreat.

"True," I told the men, "but the beauty of your words to the recipient isn't in how gloriously they're put together. The beauty is in the effort, in the feeling behind your words, in the bond that they represent. And it's simple. You can write stuff on the sticky notes, a reminder that a seemingly small gesture is actually a huge gesture."

George Bailey's final words to his father weren't the stuff of poetic beauty: "I think you're a great guy." But you have to believe that for a man who'd clearly been worn down by life—"Had another tussle with Potter today," Peter Bailey told his son earlier—and who was troubled by his son's future—"Your mother and I talked it over half the night"—George's words were reassuring.

You can imagine those words giving Pop's turbulent soul at least a temporary cease-fire, focusing his perspective on what's really important. *Potter may despise me, but I still have people close to me who love and respect me.* You can imagine them bolstering his spirit, reminding him—on what would be the night he would die—that his legacy, living on through his sons, had been an honorable one.

Don't Wait to Tell Someone You Care

Think of three people important to you. What are some small gestures you can make in the next week that will be very meaningful to them?

_____

_____

_____

_____

Read Ephesians 5:15–20. Verse 16 encourages us to "[make] the most of every opportunity." Why is it important not to put off telling someone you care?

_____

_____

_____

LESSON 18

Every Journey Has a Secret Destination

I'm going to see the world. Italy, Greece, the
Parthenon . . . the Coliseum. Then I'm coming
back here and go to college and see what they
know . . . and then I'm going to build things . . .
—George Bailey

If you had given a young George Bailey a preview of his life, shown him a newsreel of the man he would become, shown the clips of him married to Mary Hatch, father of four children, president of the Bailey Building and Loan, and above all, entrenched in the place he so desperately wanted to leave, Bedford Falls, you'd have to think he'd have mixed emotions.

The Mary-and-kids deal may have looked inviting, but staying in Bedford Falls? This is the guy who told his father no thanks to taking over the family business. He wanted to do something "big" and "important." He would have taken whatever crystal ball was being used to forecast this destiny of being stuck in his hometown and flung it aside as he did the scale model of his bridge and skyscrapers in the family living room on that life-changing Christmas Eve. Or with a quieter sense of dignity, calmly argued that, no, there must be some sort of mistake. This was George Bailey whose future you were forecasting. A guy who was going places. Doing things. Buildings bridges and airfields and skyscrapers "a hundred stories high."

But at movie's end, what George realizes is that life's road leads us to places we'd never have expected—and that's not such a bad thing at all. We might think we're going "here," but life might take us "there." As the Jewish philosopher Martin Buber says: "Every journey has a secret destination of which the traveler is unaware."

My wife and I were in Boston. The speaking event was for a hospital banquet in Boxborough, Massachusetts. Because I've never been a freeway guy, I suggested to my wife that we use "the little squiggly roads" that would take us on what looked to be a more direct route—if slower because of the curves.

We did. We soon found ourselves winding on narrow but inviting roads, houses having given way to forests. A sign fronted a small country store: "Walden Pond Market," it said. Someone, I figured, was trying to capitalize on author Henry David Thoreau to sell groceries; an irony, given that he embraced so strongly the non-materialistic world.

But as we came around the next turn, I saw it: a beautiful lake stretching out to the west. *Could this actually be it?* A rustic wooden sign answered my question soon after I'd asked it. Walden Pond, it said. Somehow, we had stumbled across the pond where the now-famous, then-obscure author had retreated in 1845 to immerse himself in the art of living simply, the result of which was his landmark book, *Walden*.

It was like a Catholic being in Italy and accidentally coming across the Vatican. Like a baseball fan being in New York state and coming across Cooperstown. Like a naturalist being in Arizona and finding himself staring down at the Grand Canyon.

Our journey had a secret destination of which neither of us, in the beginning, was aware. As did George Bailey's journey. He never went anywhere. He never built things. Heck, he couldn't even keep the staircase newel post affixed to the banister. Ah, but while Sam Wainwright was off taking the freeway to material success and brother Harry was off taking the freeway to football and war glory, George was winding his way through the squiggly lines in the forest. And there, on a Christmas Eve that began as if destined for disaster, he, too, found something wonderful that he hadn't even been looking for.

Understanding. Hope. Renewal.

Not in some far-off country such as Italy, Baghdad, or Samarkand, places he'd once told the guy in the luggage shop he wanted to visit, but in the living room of the old Granville House, surrounded by family and friends who'd gathered a wicker basket of money for him. Sure, George took a side trip through time, led by an angel named Clarence, but that had been only a means to an end, to his real "secret destination"—his Walden Pond or Cooperstown—the realization that he was the richest man in town.

Where might your life's secret destination lie? As a traveler, you'll never find out by sticking to the mundanity of the freeways.

Imagine a place you've always wanted to go but simply haven't gone yet. Similarly, are there destinations you'd like to reach on your faith journey? List them here and ask God to show you pathways to reach them.

_____

_____

_____

_____

Sometimes life's most transformational moments occur when we leave the beaten path. When did this happen in your own life, and where did you end up?

_____

_____

_____

Don't Look for What Is, but for What May Be

It's full of romance, that old place. I'd like to live in it.
—MARY, ON THE NIGHT SHE AND GEORGE THROW ROCKS
AND MAKE WISHES AT THE OLD GRANVILLE HOUSE

If George and Mary share much in common, they are different in many respects too. We learn that in one of the movie's first scenes, in which soda jerk George is waiting on a young Mary Hatch and Violet Bick. (Back in the days, apparently, when it was okay for two nine-year-old girls to be alone, downtown, and for a twelve-year-old kid to be working the front counter by himself.)

George fashions himself as a worldly young man who even

knows where coconuts come from—"Tahiti, Fiji Islands, the Coral Sea!" Mary has no idea where they come from. George wants to go exploring. Mary just wants chocolate ice cream. But here's the thing about Mary Hatch: She knows what matters. She has keen insight. Imagination. Initiative. Intuition. Perspective. And, when you boil it right down, wisdom.

And what it all seems to tell her is this: the grass isn't necessarily greener somewhere else. Why not, instead, take what you have right now, right here, and make the most of it?

We first see that in the soda shop scene. Forget ice cream. Forget the Fiji Islands. What Mary wants, among other things we can assume, is to grow up and marry George Bailey. It may only be puppy love, but when Mary whispers into George's bad ear, "I'll love you till the day I die," we're witnessing the initiative of a young woman who knows something good when she sees it. (I mean, come on; the guy eventually will be deemed the richest man in town, right?) Never mind that this model comes with its deficiencies; the kid can't hear out of one ear since he jumped into that icy pond to save his brother. Despite George's weaknesses, Mary sees something special in him.

Likewise with the Granville house. Nine years later, as George and Mary walk home from the high school dance, they come across a house that might have been nice back in its day—say, the 1890s—but wasn't looking particularly swell in 1929. "I wouldn't live in it as a ghost," says George. But Mary looks at it quite differently. "It's full of romance, that old place," she says, a smile warming her face. "I'd like to live in it." When she looked at the house, she didn't see the decrepit mess it had become. Instead she imagined how grand it one day could be. She didn't see its decay but its potential. Didn't dwell on its downtrodden past but dreamed of its glorious future.

Like God does with us. He doesn't care as much about where we've been as where we're going. About what we look like now as what we might look like in the future. About the defeats of yesterday as what might be our victories of tomorrow. With Him, all things are made new. Even decrepit folks like us.

Mary Hatch understands that the good things aren't necessarily "out there" but right here, where we live. Indeed, within us. Remember, she had gone off to college along with Sam Wainwright and Harry Bailey but tells an incredulous George that she was homesick for Bedford Falls, underscoring their differences: He wants to leave. She, having left, wants to come back. In short, Mary Hatch is a quiet guardian of sensibility who understands all that heart-trumps-the-head stuff. The "kind [of girl]," says George's mother, "that will help you find the answers."

And, of course, that's exactly what she does. She grounds George in the hearth-and-home things that matter, though willingly lets him dream, with their plans to honeymoon with a grand trip far from Bedford Falls and with George's scale models of buildings and a bridge in the family living room. And she saves the day when, during the run on the bank, she offers the honeymoon money to the customers of the Bailey Building and Loan. On the same day, with a sort of Superwoman zeal, she whips together the old Granville house into a honeymoon suite.

That scene alone underscores Mary's ability to take what life has given her and make the most of it. Amid a rainstorm the place is leaking as if built of mosquito netting, but Mary doesn't obsess about that; instead, she turns the ramshackle house into a home—in only a few short hours. She gets the bedroom ready. (After all, it is their wedding night.) She enlists Bert and Ernie to slap up some posters, a nod to her new husband's wanderlust. And then she prepares a chicken dinner, complete with a rotisserie that involves the house's fireplace and a phonograph player.

Quite simply, Mary understands that the best things in life are the simple things that surround us, especially when coupled with our imaginations. Then we can exploit those things for goodness. Why spend a lifetime searching the ends of the earth for this elusive "something," she seems to reason, when, with only a little initiative, you can take the good things you have right here and create something even better? Remember, on George's visit to her house, how she plays "Buffalo Gals" on the phonogram to stir the embers of his memories?

Imagination. Mary Hatch isn't one to simply let life "happen" to her. But neither is she one to believe that happiness is something you must pursue with some obsessive zeal for "elsewhere." And who can argue with her track record? She longs, as a nine-year-old, to spend her life with George Bailey. And does. She dreams of living in the

Granville house. And does. And on that potentially fatal Christmas Eve, she prays to get help for her distraught husband. And does.

Mary's lesson for us all is to see and to appreciate all we have in our midst. And, with God's help, to make it more than anyone else could have imagined.

Mary Bailey sees the hidden potential of the old Granville house. Imagining your own life as a house with many rooms, which rooms have potential for transformation? Which ones would you leave as is?

_____

_____

_____

_____

Mary's solid practicality is a nice counterweight for George's dreamy ambitions. Who in your life keeps you grounded and how?

_____

_____

_____

LESSON 20

It's in Helping Others That We Help Ourselves

*If I should accomplish this mission—I
mean—might I perhaps win my wings?*
—CLARENCE, TO FRANKLIN

In my many years as a journalist, among the things I've learned is
this: the people who are the most content are the ones helping others.
I've seen it time and again. In rag-tag hospitals set up in cinder block
churches in rural Haiti. In schools where teachers go the extra mile
to help kids who aren't getting much help at home. In the basement
of a church that opens its doors to homeless teenagers during the cold
winter months.

The people doing this helping were often cut from the same cloth as Clarence the Angel: quiet, unassuming folks whom some might look at as castoffs themselves. Folks not interested in impressing others. Folks with big hearts, gentle spirits, and a thirst to reach out to those who are struggling. And folks who feel as if they've been blessed through their experiences.

True, Clarence enters his mission with an ulterior motive: He wants to earn his wings. He wants a reward. But early on, it's clear that he's an angel full of compassion, empathy, and hope. And he's eager to help. In other words, he's not so focused on the reward that he overlooks that the bottom line here is *helping* a man. "Splendid!" he says when Franklin informs him that a man down on earth needs help.

When all is said and done, however, Clarence gets more than the wings he so desires. He also gets clarity of vision. At the movie's start, Clarence lacks such vision, given his superior Joseph's comment to him when he fails to see the town to which he must go. "Oh, I forgot. You haven't got your wings yet. . . . If you ever get your wings," the angel tells him, "you'll see all by yourself."

That's exactly what I've learned from the hundreds and hundreds of "givers" I've interviewed in a world full of takers: They have a clarity on life. They see a truth that the takers—the folks who believe that he who dies with the most toys wins—cannot see. And this clarity is an affirmation of Jesus' words in Acts 20:35: "It is more blessed to give than to receive."

The idea is not that we should give to others in order to receive, which, you could argue, is what Clarence is doing. But we should give because God first gave to us, and we're called to walk in His footsteps. The side benefit of blessing others is being blessed ourselves.

Remember the scene in the bridge tollhouse when George and Clarence are drying off and warming up? Clarence tells George that he has come from heaven and had to jump in the river to save George. "I knew if I were drowning you'd try to save me. And you see, you did, and that's how I saved you."

It's a fascinating dynamic at work here, this idea that helpers are helped themselves by helping. By jumping in, by taking a risk, by trying to save someone else, we are—Clarence suggests—saving ourselves.

But some people never muster the courage to jump. They're afraid of giving up familiarity for the unknown, afraid of giving up all they have for nothing that, at the moment, they can see.

In Luke 18, a rich ruler asks Jesus what he must do to inherit eternal life. Among other things, Jesus says, "[You must] sell everything you have and give [it] to the poor, and you will have treasure in heaven. Then come, follow me" (v. 22).

Lacking vision, the ruler "became very sad, because he was a man of great wealth" (v. 23). His wealth clouded his ability to see—or trust that he'd someday see—the benefits of leaving behind his materialistic life to help others.

Contrast his reaction to that of the biblical Isaiah, who, when

God asks, "Whom shall I send?" says, "Send me!" (Isaiah 6:8). Clarence, clearly, has a touch of Isaiah in him. He was ready to go, never stopping to consider what the risk might be. I mean, let's face it: he was living in heaven, a pretty cushy existence, right? And yet he was eager, even despite past failures, to go.

In the end, Clarence learns the secret lesson that all true givers learn: that, indeed, it is in giving that we receive. Though we might go into an unknown situation with a fuzzy focus, the risk we take brings us *clarity*. So the people we try to help wind up helping us.

I once spoke at a banquet involving a nonprofit program whereby adult mentors were matched with kids in rural communities who seemed to be slipping through the cracks, kids who weren't getting much support at home and needed people to come alongside them and believe in them. This was no small commitment; the adults were expected to commit to three years of mentoring these children who, at first, they only knew as troubled kids.

When one such adult was recognized with an award—in other words, "earned his wings"—he broke down at the podium. "This isn't fair," he said. "Why should I be awarded for giving so much to this kid when he gave so much more to me?"

He had experienced that wondrous thing that only those who dare to take a risk can experience: in helping others we help ourselves.

Read James 1:27. How does *charity* (the act of looking outside of ourselves and helping others in need) give us *clarity*?

_____

_____

_____

_____

Jesus said it's better to give than to receive (Acts 20:35). What are the ways that giving enriches our faith journey and draws us closer to God?

_____

_____

_____

LESSON 21

Life Is Not a Bed of Roses

Why did we have to live here in . . .
this measly, crummy old town?
—GEORGE BAILEY

I always mentally chuckle when I read some cynical piece about how *It's a Wonderful Life*, to borrow words old man Potter used in another context, is a bunch of "sentimental hogwash." Soon after the movie came out in December 1946, the *New York Times* called it "a figment of simple Pollyanna platitudes."[1] Others lamented that it was a sappy, unrealistic movie written, directed, and filmed by people wearing rose-colored glasses. "An orgy of sweetness," opined Britain's *Daily Graphic*. "This isn't a film; it's a full gale of sentiment," wrote London's *Daily Express*.

Oh, really? These are interesting observations when you really explore the nuances of George Bailey's life as portrayed in the movie. You wonder if the movie's wonderfully happy ending overshadows the darkness that's led up to that point. The broader themes touch on two historic times, neither of which qualify as particularly upbeat: the worst economic depression in US history and the most devastating war humankind has ever known.

Beyond those, however, let's focus on the more intricate themes of George Bailey himself. The film begins with a scene in which we're hearing prayers because a man is so distraught that he's left his family and wandered out into a snowstorm. We soon learn that this man, George Bailey, wants to kill himself.

Suddenly, we're flashing back to George's life as a little boy. George catches a cold while trying to save his brother from drowning in an icy pond and suffers hearing loss in one ear. It doesn't help that particular ear when his boss, Mr. Gower the druggist, slaps George so hard that it begins to bleed.

One of the happiest nights of George's life turns tragic when he learns his father has had a stroke and subsequently dies. George has a few small dreams—to travel, build things, and go to college—but everywhere he turns, such dreams are dashed. He doesn't get to go to college, doesn't get to travel, doesn't get to build anything other than the scale models of skyscrapers and a bridge in his Bedford Falls living room.

He's so lonely that while everyone celebrates the marriage of his brother, Harry, and Ruth, he wanders downtown and tries to get a date with the town floozy and is subsequently humiliated by her, much to the delight of a crowd that has gathered to laugh long, hard, and humiliatingly at Loser George.

When he stops to see Mary Hatch, her mother scorns him. When he and Mary unlock their latent desire for each other with an embrace, the eavesdropping Mrs. Hatch breaks into sobs, horrified that Mary is giving up the good life with big-city boy Sam Wainwright for this hometown nobody. After George marries Mary, he doesn't even get to go on his honeymoon because he stays to save Bailey Building and Loan during a run on the bank. (See a theme here? Happy moments dashed by hard, cold reality, hardly the stuff of sugar and spice and everything nice.) He spends his honeymoon not drinking the most expensive champagne, as he'd planned, but eating in the living room of a vacant house that he doesn't own while rain drips from a leaky roof.

The guy works his tail off to keep the family business alive. He makes forty-five dollars a week, some of which he gives to his mother. He can't afford a nice car, like the Browns's next door. He can't take time off to take Mary to Florida with Sam and his new wife, presumably on Sam's nickel. And he can't disagree with Potter when, while the banker tries to recruit him, he calls George a young man who "hates his job—who hates the Building and Loan almost as much as I do. A young man who's been dying to get out on his own ever since he was born."

George doesn't become a war hero overseas, but, instead, a lowly air-raid warden on the home front; the draft board—and Potter—finds him "4-F" because of his bad ear. When Uncle Billy loses thousands of dollars of the bank's money, George takes the blame, though nearly pummeling the old coot for his forgetfulness. He yells at his wife, yells at his kid, yells at Zuzu's schoolteacher on the phone, yells at the schoolteacher's husband. He busts up the scale models he's been working on and, for all intents and purposes, is told by Mary to hit the road.

When he does, Potter berates him as a "warped, frustrated young man," swears out a warrant for his arrest—never mind the legality of that—and phones reporters to trumpet the news of George's demise. George has a few stiff ones at Martini's and, after praying, gets clobbered by a guy at the bar who happens to be the husband of the schoolteacher he'd riddled on the phone.

Dinged by a punch and dulled by drink—no way he should have been driving—he hops in his car and rams into a tree. He then stumbles onto a bridge and, as snow swirls around him, looks furtively around him to see if anyone is watching and hunches, as if to jump.

This is an "orgy of sweetness"?

Though sweet in parts, funny in parts, and obviously upbeat at the end, it's also a bleak movie about a man who's something of a ticking time bomb, his latent rage finally exploding on Christmas Eve. In fact, one of the reasons it's believed the movie didn't do particularly well at the box office when first released was that it had been promoted as an upbeat, lighthearted love story, which is what viewers wanted in the years after World War II, but many found it too cold and dark. Too close to home.

More than half a century later, while *It's a Wonderful Life* can warm the heart, it can also remind us that, in the words of an old Amy Grant song, "life is hard . . . and it might not get easier."[2]

In spite of the disappointment, tragedy, and setbacks that George has experienced in his lifetime, what are the things that make his life decidedly worth living?

_____

_____

_____

_____

Read Luke 12:22–30. What does this passage teach us about the struggles we face in our daily lives?

_____

_____

_____

LESSON 22

It Takes a Village to Raise a Child

They're not my children.
—Mr. Potter

But they're somebody's children.
—Peter Bailey

It's a Wonderful Life is not only a movie about a man, George Bailey. It's a movie about a place, Bedford Falls, which, in essence, becomes a character in the story. The town, we're shown, has a personality that changes dramatically depending on who ushers its destiny— the Baileys or Potter. It changes costumes depending on the season, director Frank Capra deepening the story with snow, wind, rain, and sunshine. It seems to have a collective personality, say, during the run-on-the-bank scene, when masses show up for their money and, after a siren goes off—an impromptu addition by director Capra, by the way—they shuffle to the window, as if one, to look. Bedford Falls is portrayed as a battler, a brawler, and a town that some want to leave for better things. But largely because of the Baileys, it's also seen as a nourishing place that takes care of its own.

The scene that cements this comes early in the movie when Potter and Peter Bailey are sparring as a young George shows up for advice about the poisoned-pill incident. Potter suggests Peter isn't putting enough pressure on people to pay their rents. But times are tough, the Building and Loan founder points out.

"Then foreclose!" says Potter.

"I can't do that," Peter objects. "These families have children."

"They're not my children," harrumphs Potter.

"But they're *somebody's* children," maintains Peter.

In this single exchange, we see how two men look at the same circumstances through such different eyes. Potter sees children as an afterthought, a nuisance, someone else's problem. Peter sees them as important, integral to the town, and his opportunity to help. In so doing, he underscores the idea that it takes a village to raise a child, though it's almost become a cliché in our twenty-first century.

To Potter, children are just in the way. It takes a discerning eye, but in the opening sledding scene, a sign right behind George, as brother Harry zips down the hill, warns, "No Trespassing—Henry F. Potter." In fact, until Capra changed it just before shooting, the scene was much longer and, more significantly, opens with the boys playing hockey right next to Potter's prisonlike house, from which someone has unleashed "vicious dogs" that charge the boys and lead to Harry breaking through the ice.

In the Bailey world, of course, children are important. They're taken seriously. George is only twelve when he's working the soda shop alone. They're honored by adults. The dance scene suggests a tight bond between school administrators and students. Even Violet Bick seems to get along with the senior-citizen principal, Mr. Partridge, who must be her grandfather's age. When he taps her on the shoulder to suggest she and her partner can remain in the Charleston contest, he also appears to lightheartedly scold her, pointing at what he considers a too-short skirt. But she gives him a smiling hug in return. Heck, when the gym floor opens and kids start splashing into the pool, even Mr. Partridge eventually gives in to the spirit of fun and dives in.

In the scene involving the dedication of the Martini house, George mirrors his father's respect for young people. Can you imagine Potter, even if he were able to walk, helping usher children and their goat into the backseat of a car?

The point is that the movie exudes a collective message that children matter and it's up to adults to guide, encourage, and celebrate them. That's as important now, whatever community we live in, as it was back then in Bedford Falls.

It Takes a Village to Raise a Child

Jesus cared deeply for children, which likely surprised His contemporaries. Read Mark 10:13–16. What does it mean to "receive the kingdom of God like a little child"?

_____

_____

_____

_____

Think of a child or young person who is significant in your life. What are some ways you can uplift and encourage them this week?

_____

_____

_____

LESSON 23

Quiet Lives Can Speak the Loudest

*You know, George, I feel that in a small way we are
doing something important. Satisfying a fundamental
urge. It's deep in the race for a man to want his own
roof and walls and fireplace, and we're helping
him get those things in our "shabby little office."*
—PETER BAILEY

George thinks big. And, really, what's wrong with that? Ambition, when focused on the right things, is a good thing, right? The world needs visionaries, dreamers who imagine making something out of nothing, making more out of less, making changes for the better. (God thinks big about making us more than we are, doesn't He?) Beyond his desire to design new buildings and plan modern cities,

George is the guy, after all, who tells Sam Wainwright that his father ought to locate his new plastics plant right there in Bedford Falls.

But the spotlight is not necessarily better than the shadows. Scripture is full of in-the-shadows folks whom God esteems highly, from a shepherd boy, David, to a widow who gives her all with a single mite. Likewise, *It's a Wonderful Life* makes a quiet pitch for the little guy, the behind-the-scenes person who makes the world a better place with no fanfare or trumpets. In the dinner scene in the Bailey home before the dance, Peter Bailey suggests as much while talking to George about his son possibly taking over the family business. The idea, of course, bombs with George, who retorts with his biting lines about how he'd go crazy working in that "shabby little office" in this "business of nickels and dimes . . . I want to do something big and something important."

To which Peter Bailey responds with what, in keeping with the very point he's making, is one of those quiet but incisive nuggets of wisdom the movie offers: "You know, George, I feel that in a small way we are doing something important. Satisfying a fundamental urge. It's deep in the race for a man to want his own roof and walls and fireplace, and we're helping him get those things in our 'shabby little office.'"

In other words, the good we bring to the world, to the community, to our families, doesn't necessarily have to be big and glitzy. It can be small and quiet, which doesn't negate its importance.

Let's take teachers. They rarely get praised. They operate, for the most part, out of the public spotlight. The bulk of them rarely make headlines. But in a small way they are doing something extremely important: helping mold the lives of young people.

Let's take missionaries. The existence many of them live would make a "shabby little office" seem like a king's palace. And yet they toil in obscurity to reach people with God's love.

Let's take mothers and fathers. Parenting is often one of those "nickel-and-dime" jobs, the day-to-day challenge of helping bring up young people who can be fickle, who are always changing, who are craving independence even as they're craving the security of home. But how mind-blowing to think that we, as parents, will be the biggest influence on who they will become.

Finally, let's take folks who work jobs that might not seem particularly significant, in the same way George didn't think his father's job was especially significant. Perhaps one of the keys to finding satisfaction in our lives is perspective, looking at the world through the people-oriented glasses of Peter Bailey, who, despite the constant battles with Potter, took pride in what he and his small business did for the good people of Bedford Falls. Who was a man of substance, not style. Who understood that quiet lives can still speak so loudly.

Quiet Lives Can Speak the Loudest

Think of people you know who work quietly behind the scenes, making a difference in the lives of others, often without praise or reward. List them here and offer up brief prayers, thanking God for their service.

_____

_____

_____

_____

Read Matthew 6:1–8. What does this passage reveal about "[practicing] your righteousness in front of others"?

_____

_____

_____

LESSON 24

No Man Is an Island

We can get through this thing all right.
We've got to stick together, though. We've
got to have faith in each other.
—GEORGE BAILEY

In the bank-run scene, George tries to still the hysteria by encouraging people not to panic; to panic, he said, would be to play right into the hands of old man Potter. But he also suggests their survival depends on something else: understanding that they're all in this together. That, essentially, the whole is stronger than the individual. That they need each other.

The metaphor he uses to make a deeper point is money. When people demand to withdraw their funds, George points out that it's not as if the money is all sitting in a safe. "The money's not here. Your money's in Joe's house . . . right next to yours. And in the Kennedy house, and Mrs. Macklin's house, and a hundred others . . . Now what are you going to do?" he asks. "Foreclose [on your neighbors to get what belongs to you]?"

Whether the group is a church, community, family, business, military outfit, or whatever, its strength always depends on it understanding its commitment to one another. Understanding that the individual is strengthened by its dependency on the group. Understanding that, in the end, no man is an island.

I had the privilege of writing a book about one of World War II's "Band of Brothers." Don Malarkey was part of Easy Company, the 101st Airborne unit whose story was told in a book by Stephen Ambrose (*Band of Brothers*) and in the ten-part HBO series of the same name produced by Steven Spielberg and Tom Hanks.

I remember Malarkey telling me about the aftermath of a shelling his unit took in the Battle of the Bulge, which played out in the haunting cold and snow of Bastogne, Belgium. The legs of two buddies had been blown off. Malarkey confessed that, while standing around a campfire with a handful of other guys, his spirits were so low that he considered putting a bullet in his foot so he would be of no use to the unit and would be sent back to England. It was not, he admitted, a particularly noble thought, but in times of despair, men sometimes think ignoble thoughts.

"I know you didn't shoot yourself, Don," I said. "Why not?"

Because, he told me in so many words, he realized he was necessary to the others. Most of the unit's leadership was dead or wounded. If he were to leave, too, it would be better for him but worse for the whole.

It's the same message George is trying to get the Building and Loan customers to appreciate: that their survival depends on individuals making sacrifices for the betterment of the group. Sure, to withdraw their money—what little there was—would have been better for them individually; but it would have been worse for the whole.

The key to survival is trusting the power of the group, he suggests. "We can get through this thing all right," he says. "We've got to stick together, though. We've got to have faith in each other."

Churches would do well to heed the message; how many have splintered into selfish factions because their members underestimated the importance of unity?

Families would do well to heed the message; how many have been torn apart by parents or children looking out only for themselves, not the group?

Any organization would do well to heed the message; how many once-proud businesses or nonprofits died from within, eaten by the insidious bug of greed instead of flourishing because of people who understood that the unit's real power rested in their willingness to stick together and to have faith in each other.

"Live in peace with each other," wrote Paul. "And we urge you, brothers, warn those who are idle, encourage the timid, help the weak, be patient with everyone" (1 Thessalonians 5:13–14).

In other words, learn to get along with each other so you might all flourish.

Consider all the communities you encounter on a weekly basis: work, school, church, family, social groups, and so forth. How are these groups made stronger by unity versus self-interest?

_____

_____

_____

_____

Living in peace with others can often be challenging in today's world. Who is someone you've had conflict with in your life? What are some ways you can reach out and heal wounds to bring about peace?

_____

_____

_____

LESSON 25

God's Greatest Gift Is Life

*At exactly ten-forty-five PM tonight, Earth
time, that man will be thinking seriously
of throwing away God's greatest gift.*
—FRANKLIN'S VOICE

Oh, dear, dear! His life!
—CLARENCE'S VOICE

It's a Wonderful Life—even the title suggests it—is a life-affirming story. At its core, it's a story about how precious life is and how what we get out of it depends so much on how much we value it. How we live life. What we give back to our lives.

The irony, of course, is that the guy who seems to live life best is also the guy who's standing on that snowy bridge on Christmas Eve, considering throwing his life away. And it's not until Clarence, in effect, temporarily takes away his life that George understands what it's all about. So he proclaims, "I want to live again. I want to live again. Please, God, let me live again."

The message is this: living life the right way begins with an appreciation for what we have. An understanding of how precious life is. An attitude for living life to its fullest. That's what we're meant to do. "I have come that they may have life, and have it to the full," said Jesus in John 10:10.

And what does that fullness of life hinge on? Strangely enough, the scripture suggests, on giving it away. "The reason my Father loves me," He said, "is that I lay down my life—only to take it up again" (John 10:17). It's in giving that we receive. In sacrifice that we realize life to the fullest. "Greater love has no one than this, that he lay down his life for his friends" (John 15:13). In lifting up others, we find the essence of ourselves.

Isn't this the way George Bailey has lived his entire life? In the first scene, he lays down his life for his brother—risks death to save Harry. And in less dramatic but no less profound ways, he keeps doing that the rest of the movie, whether it's giving up his and Mary's honeymoon nest egg so people won't defect to Potter during the bank run, giving up his dreams so Harry can go off to college, or giving from his own wallet so Violet Bick can get a start in New York.

But the movie suggests that "doing good works" is empty

without an understanding of the importance of such good works in the context of fullness of life. Isn't that why George is considering suicide? Even though he has lived his life for others, he doesn't recognize the value of his own life—that it is God's greatest gift, and that in living it for others, he has experienced a life well lived.

In many ways, George Bailey's role model for life is his father. In the bank-run scene, as George is trying to quell the crowd of people who have come to withdraw their money, he glances at the wall and sees the quote from the man: "All you can take with you is that which you've given away." And George certainly seems to live his life with that same spirit. But the Christmas Eve scene suggests that George has been living with his head, not his heart, and thereby missing the life-affirming essence of his father's words.

It's as if he's become the church attender who puts his money in the plate each week, but his heart's not in it; the do-the-right-thing guy who nevertheless forgets that God wants our attitudes to come along with our actions: "God loves a cheerful giver" (2 Corinthians 9:7). It's not that George has become overly proud in his giving, like some Pharisee, wanting to give and let it be known that he's done so. It's that he's lost the *purpose* in giving, lost what Clarence helps him find: the understanding that giving isn't just the right thing to do; it's living life at its deepest. Its fullest. Its most meaningful.

When Clarence reminds him of this, he finds a deeper sense of purpose. As he runs through the streets of Bedford Falls, wishing strangers a "Merry Christmas," as he embraces his children, as he showers Mary with kisses, it's as if he's not just doing good things; George Bailey is finally living life to its fullest.

The movie pointedly suggests throughout that the thing that enriches life the most is sacrifice. Who made sacrifices in your life, and how was your life enriched by those actions?

_____

_____

_____

_____

Who in your circle of friends needs life-affirming encouragement this week? What ways can you help them recognize the value of their own life?

_____

_____

_____

LESSON 26

The Greatest Gift You Can Give Is Grace

Here, Ed. You remember last year when things
weren't going so well, and you couldn't make your
payments? You didn't lose your house, did you?
Do you think Potter would have let you keep it?
—George Bailey

Grace—undeserved favor—is a Bailey trademark. Think about all the times George or his father grants grace to other people. George's druggist boss slaps him so hard his bad ear starts bleeding. Goodness! If not an assault charge, that's a lawsuit waiting to happen, but George understands the man's anger: "You got that telegram." Peter

Bailey's Building and Loan customers owe him money, and Potter wants him to foreclose on them, but Peter overlooks their debt.

George follows in his father's footsteps in this regard. In trying to get the people to understand that they're safer keeping their money with the Bailey Building and Loan than getting fifty cents on the dollar at the bank, George suggests that one reason to do so is that the Baileys believe in grace and Potter doesn't: "Here, Ed. You remember last year when things weren't going so well, and you couldn't make your payments? You didn't lose your house, did you? Do you think Potter would have let you keep it?" The Baileys routinely do something for others that they don't have to do: give them favor that, legally, they aren't bound to do.

How about grace when it comes to Uncle Billy and the eight grand he lost to Potter? Granted, his nephew roughs him up a bit when the old coot can't find the dough, but after George flees the family on Christmas Eve and goes to Potter for a loan, he lies to protect the guy. "I've just misplaced eight thousand dollars," he tells Potter. "I can't find it anywhere." George takes responsibility for the lost money and, in so doing, lets Uncle Billy off the hook.

Grace is the foundation of the Christian faith. Jesus' granting us grace by forgiving our sins flies in the face of virtually every other religion, which operates on a you-get-what-you-deserve basis. But Jesus says, in essence, you don't get what you deserve. You get what you *don't* deserve. You're redeemable even if you've blown it.

Against the backdrop of such amazing love, the biggest shame of the Christian faith is believers who've been granted such grace but who, in turn, treat others without grace. No mercy. The template for such behavior is outlined in Matthew 18. A king wants to settle his accounts with his servants. A man who owes him ten thousand talents, about $1 million, is brought before the master. Because the servant can't pay, he's told that he and his wife and children will be sold to repay the debt.

"Be patient with me," the servant begs, "and I will pay back everything."

The master takes pity on him, cancels the debt, and lets him go.

The servant's response? "He found one of his fellow servants who owed him a hundred denarii [a denarius was a day's pay, so one hundred days' pay]. He grabbed him and began to choke him. 'Pay back what you owe me!' he demanded" (v. 28).

It would be like George telling Uncle Billy, "Look, pal, that money got lost on *your* watch, so you're fired, and you need to pay it all back. Pronto." Uncle Billy pleads for mercy, and George, discarding his Potteresque facade, says, "Aw, shucks, forget it. You're family." Uncle Billy then wanders down to Martini's and finds himself sitting next to a Bailey Park homeowner who's three months overdue on his mortgage. Pinning the guy to the jukebox, he says, "Pay up, pal, or we'll send out Nick as a convincer."

Grace sometimes explodes in front of us as magnificently as fireworks and sometimes arrives as gently as a summer breeze. In the movie, you see it not only in the Baileys' patience with

Depression-racked customers, not only in George's taking the rap for Uncle Billy's misdeed, but also in quieter ways, particularly at the end.

In that final scene, the sheriff tears up the warrant for George's arrest. (Never mind the illegality of the warrant in the first place, Potter having been the author of it. A judicial officer has the power to swear out an arrest warrant, but not an ordinary citizen. Oh, well.) That's grace.

The bank examiner—who, at this point, remember, has no knowledge of how the Baileys came up eight thousand bucks short—joins in the festivities and makes a donation to George's cause, even joins in on "Hark! The Herald Angels Sing." That's grace.

Heck, even Mr. Welch, who was angry enough at George to punch him out in Martini's Bar for insulting his wife on the phone, shows up in the Bailey living room, his very presence a sign that he's cut George some slack. (You see him just over Ernie's right shoulder as the cab driver is reading the telegram from Sam Wainwright.) That's grace.

And here's a final touch of grace that might be easily missed: Mary's. Remember the context here. Regardless of what's bugging him, George, earlier, had pretty much ruined Christmas Eve for the whole Bailey family. He'd yelled at his kids, snapped at Mary, embarrassed her with his dressing down of Zuzu's teacher and her husband on the phone, even made a mess of the house. If anyone had reason not to cut slack to her husband, it was Mary Bailey on Christmas Eve.

But in the depth of her despair—remember, she all but tells George to take a hike—what does she do instead of taking the kids to her mom's house, filing for divorce, and setting his balsa-wood dreams on fire? She prays. She starts making phone calls to encourage others to help George. And, presumably, in so doing, she learns from Uncle Billy about the missing money and throws together the impromptu fundraiser.

What she really does—the umbrella over this goodness—is this: she gives George something he didn't deserve: grace. In so doing, she reminds us all of an even greater grace available for we who are equally undeserving. A grace so incredible that, when given it, we dare not dishonor it by our unwillingness to do the same for others.

The Greatest Gift You Can Give Is Grace

The author defines grace as "undeserved favor." Have you ever received grace instead of what you really deserved? What did you learn from the situation?

_____

_____

_____

_____

Who needs a little grace in the upcoming month? What are some of the ways you can express this act of kindness?

_____

_____

_____

There's Much to Be Said for Long-Term Commitments

George Bailey, I'll love you till the day I die.
—A YOUNG MARY BAILEY IN THE SODA SHOP

We live in a world where commitment, long-term commitment, has become like the eight-track tape player of personal values. Obsolete. Like hummingbirds, some of us flit from job to job, relationship to relationship, place to place—in some cases, from value system to value system.

Ever been to a garage sale and seen the array of discarded exercise equipment? You feel like an archaeologist, sifting through the remains of different workout eras—the Trampoline Era, the Bowflex

Era, the StairMaster Era. After a while, you get that the problem here wasn't the equipment but the person who bought it and apparently gave up his or her commitment to using it.

Mary Hatch isn't that way. In *It's a Wonderful Life*, she is a tortoise among hares. (How she kindled even a long-distance romance with Sam Wainwright is beyond me, given that he was just the opposite, rocketing through life with a bag of money in one hand and a dame on the other arm.) We understand this in the movie's second scene, when Mary and Violet Bick are being waited on by a young George in the soda shop.

"George Bailey," Mary whispers in his bad ear, "I'll love you till the day I die."

In other words, "I'm committed to a long-term operation here. I don't need to play the field my whole life. I'm content with settling down with the right man, even if the first thing he calls me is 'brainless.'" She waits more than a decade for George to finally wake up and realize that she's the one for him too.

She is the same way about the Granville house. She loved the old weather-beaten place from the moment she laid eyes on it, even if George didn't think it was fit for a ghost. She was so committed to it that she was willing to wait for the chance to live in it. It was 1929 when she and George threw "wish" rocks at the house on their way home from the dance. George and Mary get married in June 1932, so she waits at least three years for her dream house.

Today, ever-faster technology has made the idea of waiting

almost obsolete. We want everything, and we don't want to wait for it. Perhaps you've heard the Prayer of the Impatient: "Lord, grant me patience—and I want it right now!" Or seen the cartoon of the woman strolling down the microwave food aisle in the grocery store. "Naw," she says, "I don't have time to cook tonight." We've lost the concept of long-term commitment.

Consider the World War II generation. Those people understood long-term commitment. It wasn't uncommon for newly married husbands and wives to go years without seeing each other while the husband fought overseas. And, true, not everybody made good on their commitments. But most did. Most waited. Why? Because they understood the value of waiting.

Our willingness to wait for something indicates, at the rubber-meets-the-road level, how much we value that something. I met a young woman only weeks before I was to leave for college. And we had to make a choice: Are we in this for the long haul? The easier answer would have been no. It would have saved us lots of commuting, lots of letter writing, lots of high-low weeks filled with frustration and tears. But we chose yes. It was not an easy three years at all, but the short-term pain resulted in long-term gain: thirty-six years of marriage, two kids, four grandchildren, and thousands of dog-eared letters from the 1970s that we don't have the heart to part with.

Why? Because it was the struggle, referred to often in those letters, that steeled our relationship. That taught us patience and perseverance. That grew our characters. And you don't develop that stuff if you're not willing to make long-term commitments.

You get the idea that if a sequel to the movie had been made—say, *It's a Wonderful Life II*—George and Mary would have still been living in the Granville house, grandkids probably using the staircase newel to play soccer in the living room.

But they would have been content, realizing the value of not flitting from one thing to another but sticking with what works.

We live in a fast-paced world where technology grants us access to almost everything in a matter of seconds. Assess some areas in your life where you need to slow down, list them here, and say a brief prayer asking God to help you apply the brakes.

_____

_____

_____

_____

Have you ever been disappointed by not making a long-term commitment to some endeavor or someone? How can God help you stay the course and remain devoted?

_____

_____

_____

Actions Speak Louder Than Words

My office instructed to advance you up
to twenty-five thousand dollars.
—Telegram from Sam Wainwright

In a movie whose ending ascends from one lump-in-the-throat moment to another, this one is among the lumpiest: George's friends and family have gathered in the Bailey living room on Christmas Eve to present him with a wad of cash and a reminder that he's deeply loved.

The revelry escalates quickly. As people step forward to pour cash at George's feet, Ernie the cab driver quiets the crowd. "Just a minute. Quiet, everybody. Quiet—quiet. Now, this is from London: 'Mr. Gower cables you need cash. Stop. My office instructed to advance you up to twenty-five thousand dollars. Stop. Hee-haw and Merry Christmas. Sam Wainwright.'"

George, holding Zuzu, bows his head in—what?—gratitude, disbelief, humble appreciation, you name it. This is no small gesture. After all, $8,000—the amount the Building and Loan is short—is a lot of money. It's true, amid the pile of cash that Cousin Eustace is busily trying to total on the adding machine, a couple of $100 bills and a $1,000 bill have been donated. But if, as it appears, there are about three dozen people who show up with offerings, that's still $222 per person, which ain't chump change.

But Sam's $25,000 offer—even if the word *advance* suggests it's a loan and not a gift—soars above all others for a couple of reasons. First, the amount. It's more than three times what's missing at the Bailey Building and Loan. It assures George that the company's financial ship will be righted. More important, it comes from a guy who—if still a Bedford Falls man and not a Pottersville goon at heart—lives far beyond the humdrum ways of the small town he left.

Remember, this is Sam Wainwright, a man who called Mary from a New York office while a woman in a white mink stole teases him from behind. A man who, though not even thirty years old, has his own chauffeur and can afford to zip down to Florida for a vacation on a whim. And, not incidentally, once a suitor for the hand of the woman whom George marries. Even if Sam appears to be hee-hawing around with other women, we can assume his phone call to Mary that night was for reasons beyond an investment opportunity involving soybeans. And shortly before that, in the scene outside Harry and Ruth's party, George tells his mother he wouldn't pursue Mary because Sam Wainwright has his eye on her.

Though obviously a good-hearted guy, Sam is, at least materialistically speaking, the anti-George. He's New York; George is Bedford Falls. He's big-time; George is small-time. He's wealthy; George lives in a refurbished wreck of a house and doesn't drive a car as nice as the Browns' next door. But the interesting thing is that though Sam could have left George behind along with the rest of Bedford Falls, he has too much respect for his pal to do so.

Though en route to Florida, he takes time to swing by and say hello to George and Mary after the Martinis' house is dedicated. He trusts George's judgment, following up on his friend's suggestion to anchor his father's new plant in Bedford Falls. You get the idea that even if Sam lives a far different life than George—even if he calls him "old moss-back George," the guy who never went anywhere far or did anything big—he nevertheless has deep respect for the man. You have to wonder, amid his highbrow lifestyle, if Sam secretly admires George's bedrock values and maybe even sometimes thinks, *I wish I were more like George.*

How else do you explain his offering George such a large sum of money after Mr. Gower has wired him about "Moss-back's" troubles? Even though Sam never benefited directly from George's generosity, that generosity seems to have inspired the man to help out his buddy when he's in a pinch. Even though he's not part of the day-to-day

Bedford Falls rhythm, Sam realizes that George is, indeed, the soul of the community, and honors him for that through his gift.

The point: People are watching us. People notice. We can inspire people even if they aren't the direct recipients of our goodness. If you think about it, those who step forward to bestow their financial donations on George in this final scene are cut from two cloths. Some, indeed, have benefited directly from George's kindness. "I wouldn't have a roof over my head if it wasn't for you, George," a man says. Mr. Gower contributes, we can assume, in part because a young George saved him from accidentally poisoning a child; Mr. Martini because, thanks to George, "no more we liva like pigs in thisa Potter's Field." Violet Bick, too, returns some of the kindness George gave to her.

But the others—Mr. Partridge, the school principal; Annie, the Baileys' maid; the sheriff; and, most notably, the present-in-spirit Sam Wainwright—give because they have seen George in action and simply want to honor his example.

Why? Because actions *do* speak louder than words.

What does *It's a Wonderful Life* say about generosity? Why is generosity important in our interactions with others?

_____

_____

_____

_____

What does the Bible say about generosity? Start with these Scriptures: Psalm 112:5, Proverbs 19:17, Luke 6:38, Hebrews 13:16; 1 John 3:17.

_____

_____

_____

Look for the Best in People

Here, now, you're broke, aren't you?
—George, as he reaches in his pocket for
some money to give to Violet Bick

Violet Bick is Bedford Falls' bad girl. In looking for the right person to play the part in the movie, director Frank Capra told Jimmy Stewart, who plays George: "She has to be sultry! She must be beautiful, too, because she'll be vying with Donna Reed for your love. But she can't be a big-town siren. She's got to have a small-town goodness about her." Stewart, Capra remembered, replied: "I see. She's a good girl, but willing to be bad for the right guy."

Is she a prostitute? Capra leaves that up to our imagination in the life-with-George segments of the movie, though certainly ramps up the possibilities in the life-without-George segment. You have to remember that this movie was made in 1946 when the Motion Picture Association of America's Production Code was well known for what we'd consider now to be bizarre restrictions. Words such as *jerk*, *impotent*, *dang*, and *lousy* had to be omitted. Amid such restrictions, the scene in which George wanders downtown after leaving Harry and Ruth's party and runs into Vi raises questions. In the script, she's supposed to be closing down "Violet Bick's Beauty Shop,"[1] though that's not how it was filmed.

Instead, she is dressed for a night on the town and is being "courted" by two slick guys who don't look as if they have the library in mind. Violet sees George. "I think I got a date. But stick around, fellows, just in case, huh?"

"We'll wait for you, baby," says one of the guys.

It's just a short scene, but you can read a lot from it: (1) If Violet suddenly thinks she has a date, then apparently that's *not* what Violet had with these guys. So, exactly what *did* she have with these guys? Hmmm. (2) The relationship between the guys and Violet has a hint of "serious business" to it. And (3) whatever she has with these guys, she's more than willing to give it up for George—and her come-on line suggests she's well past her soda-shop innocence.

When George tells her that he might wander down to the library, she says, "George, don't you ever get tired of just reading about things?" (Says the script: "Her eyes are seductive and guileful as she looks up at him."[2])

Face it: this is a crossroads for George. Here's a time when Vi may be a "good girl," but is "willing to be bad for the right guy." He's well aware of Vi's beauty and magnetism; remember that scene when she walks down the street and he says, "Hey, you look good. That's some dress you got on there." And emotionally, he could use a pick-me-up; he's at one of the low points of his life, having just left a party where his brother is being feted for a new marriage that promises to foil, once again, any hopes George has of living his dreams.

But what does he do? With a guise of seriousness, he spins a bizarre story about taking Vi to the actual Bedford Falls, swimming, and hiking to the top of Mount Bedford, which turns her off like a faucet. (Am I the only one who thinks it strange how nobody is around the pair as he begins his wacky suggestion and, thirty seconds later, a dozen people are ringing around them as if they've been beamed down from another planet?) In other words, he purposely sabotages his chances for a night with a woman who's been interested in him for years.

Why? First, we can surmise, because he has a high set of moral standards for himself. But, more subtly, because he has a high set of moral standards for others too. In essence, he has too much respect for Violet Bick to take advantage of her. If that sounds odd, so be it, but one of George's attributes is that, with rare exceptions (Potter comes to mind) he looks for the good in other people.

If you're looking for a scriptural analogy, Violet Bick might be the woman at the well in John 4, a woman revered by men for her sexuality but scorned by the rest of the people for her lack of purity. But Jesus sees beyond the woman's label to her very soul, to the stuff that matters more, to her deepest needs.

Likewise, George fits into neither category, not pursuing Violet but not scorning her either. On Christmas Eve some thirteen years later, he not only loans her money from the Building and Loan but digs into his own pocket to help her out as she prepares to move to New York. He doesn't lecture her, tell her it's time she made something of her life, make her feel guilty for leaving Bedford Falls. Why? Because, at heart, he believes in her. He respects her.

And, later, we're reminded that that respect made a difference in Violet Bick. In the life-without-George sequence, Violet is downtown, struggling to resist being thrown into a patrol wagon by no fewer than four cops. (The script describes her as a "tart," or prostitute.[3]) Though difficult to hear her, what she says is, "That sailor's a liar! I know every big shot in this town! I know Potter and I'll have you kicked off the . . ."

How does she know these "big shots"? How does she know Potter? It's fairly obvious that, without George, Bedford Falls became a tougher, meaner place where people don't necessarily look for the best in each other. And Violet Bick was more than just a flirt.

But with George in the world, things are different. Violet is calmer. More focused. And after George's generosity at the Building and Loan, she later decides not to move to New York. On Christmas

Eve, with everyone gathered in the Bailey living room, she returns the money he'd given her, saying she has changed her mind.

Why? You have to wonder if George—as a sort of small-town icon—reminds her of the good people she'd be leaving; grounds her in some way; teaches her, by staying in town himself, that the grass isn't always greener on the other side. And the respect she has for him began with the respect he had for her—his willingness to see the best in her.

The author writes that Jesus sees beyond the labels placed on us by others and ourselves into our very soul. What are some of your deepest needs that you need to bring before the Lord?

_____

_____

_____

_____

An old saying goes, "You can't judge a book by its cover." Are there people or situations that you initially misjudged? How did your mindset change when you learned the truth?

_____

_____

_____

LESSON 30

Vengeance Is Not Ours, Saith the Lord

What's the matter, Othello—jealous? Did you know there's a swimming pool under this floor? And did you know that button behind you causes this floor to open up? And did you further know that George Bailey is dancing right over that crack? And I've got the key?
—MICKEY, TO FREDDIE, AT THE SCHOOL DANCE, AFTER GEORGE CUTS IN ON THE LATTER'S DANCE WITH MARY

In the years after the movie came out, director Frank Capra received an increasingly large amount of mail regarding *It's a Wonderful Life* until his death in 1991. The number one topic: How could old man

Potter (Lionel Barrymore) go unpunished after stealing eight thousand dollars from Uncle Billy?

It is a legitimate question. When the movie was made in the 1940s, the Motion Picture Production Code definitely stipulated that criminals must be punished for their crimes. Michael Willian, an attorney and author of *The Essential It's a Wonderful Life*, ponders what, exactly, Potter's crime might have been. "Larceny," he wrote, "is the best bet. While it's true that Potter did not physically take the money from Uncle Billy, the law nevertheless considers mislaid property to be constructively in the possession of its rightful owner, i.e., Uncle Billy (or more precisely, the Building and Loan). Thus, when a person finds mislaid property and retains it despite knowing full well who the rightful owner is, the crime of larceny can arise."[1]

The prosecution, of course, could argue that while Potter didn't actually take the money, his not giving it back not only constituted theft but nearly cost a man his life. (Though, of course, George would have been hesitant to admit to a judge or jury that he had almost attempted suicide.)

Capra, at a Q&A session in 1968, was asked about Potter not paying any price for his conniving ways. "What to do with Lionel Barrymore really came up at the time we were shooting it, at the time we were writing the script," he said. "How do you handle a guy like that? Well, we just left him alone. We just let him go on about his business. He was the kind of guy who wouldn't change, couldn't change. So we just left him, and our main interest was what happened to George Bailey. This Lionel Barrymore character was too crusty, too old, too happy with what he was doing to change. So we just left him as he was."

No consequences for Mr. Potter. No arrest. No trial. No nothing. Is this fair? The Scriptures suggest it's not for us to worry about. "Do not take revenge, my friends," wrote the apostle Paul, "but leave room for God's wrath, for it is written: 'It is mine to avenge; I will repay,' says the Lord. . . . Do not be overcome by evil, but overcome evil with good" (Romans 12:19, 21).

And, really, isn't that the message that exudes from the Bailey living room late on that Christmas Eve? Good *has* overcome evil. George's redemption lay in the goodness that was returned to him as a result of his goodness to others. And Potter, meanwhile, is left to wallow in a loneliness born of his selfish desires.

Given as much, perhaps the ending provides justice after all, though we can hope that in a sequel, Potter, like Charles Dickens's Scrooge, would see the light.

Have you ever wanted to get back at someone for something they said or did? How did that situation play out? Why should we leave vengeance up to the Lord?

_____

_____

_____

_____

What is the difference between revenge and justice? What are some creative ways Mr. Potter could have received justice for keeping the lost $8,000?

_____

_____

_____

Nobody Is Perfect . . . Which Brings Us to Grace

HARRY BAILEY, 1911–1919
—THE INACCURATE LIFE SPAN OF HARRY BAILEY, ON HIS
HEADSTONE, IN CLARENCE'S WORLD WITHOUT GEORGE

You have to look closely and ponder for a moment, but one of the movie's gaffes comes in the life-without-George graveyard scene. Remember? Clarence takes George to the town cemetery and shows him the headstone of his brother, Harry Bailey, who, without George around to save him, drowned in that icy pond "at the age of nine." But if Harry was born in 1911, as the tombstone says, he would not turn nine until 1920. And yet the marker indicates he died in 1919.

Imperfections abound in the production of the movie—and, of course, in the movie itself. According to newspaper accounts, when filming the scene of a tipsy Uncle Billy leaving Harry and Ruth's party while singing "My Wild Irish Rose," someone on the set accidentally knocked over a stack of props. It sounds as if Billy has tripped over a couple of garbage cans full of bottles. However, quick-on-his-feet actor Thomas Mitchell took advantage of the miscue, saying back to George, "I'm all right, I'm all right." Not only did it work wonderfully, but the guilty party, instead of being reprimanded or fired, was given a ten-dollar reward by Capra for "improving sound and characterization." Or so the story goes.

And really, why, on Christmas Eve 1945—the year World War II ended—is Potter still traveling by horse-drawn carriage? You'll just catch a glimpse of it as Potter enters the bank, right before Uncle Billy unknowingly slips him the eight grand. We hadn't seen that get-up in a movie since 1919 and, in the decades since, the country has switched from horses to cars.

Yep, the movie has flaws. On Christmas Eve day, George enters the Building and Loan with a Christmas wreath on his arm. On hearing that he has a phone call from his brother, Harry, he tosses the wreath on a table and picks up the phone. In the next second, the wreath is back on his arm. Go figure.

The people in the movie also have flaws. George has a latent temper, and to a lesser degree, so does Mary. (How about that "Buffalo Gals" record she shatters?) Uncle Billy forgets nearly everything he tries to remember. Peter Bailey has a big heart, but even George admits he was "no business man." Mr. Gower, the druggist, has a mean streak, especially when drinking. (Just ask George's ear.) And Violet apparently hasn't had many positive male influences in her life.

The bottom line: nobody is good enough, not even the "good" people. And don't even get me started on old man Potter, a selfish opportunist who will exploit anyone—even children!—for a buck. "For all have sinned," says Romans 3:23, "and fall short of the glory of God." But if not even the "good" people in life are good enough, it would seem that even if we aspire to live the upright life of a George Bailey or Mary Bailey, we're all destined to live guilt-ridden lives on earth because of our shortcomings, dying with no chance for redemption.

Ah, but here's where God's grace comes into play.

It begins with the realization that He loves us in a way the world does not: unconditionally. Without an agenda. With no fine print that says He loves us now, but it's only an introductory-rate offer that will change after six months based on prime interest rates. With no campaign promise that He'll love us, but only if we vote for Him or give to His campaign fund. With no prenuptial agreement that says He'll love us, but, just in case, let's put together a contract.

It ends with a promise that eternal life awaits not those who live perfect lives, say so many Hail Marys, never miss church, or donate so much money, but to those who *believe* with childlike faith. "For it is by grace you have been saved, through faith—and this not from yourselves, it is the gift of God" (Ephesians 2:8).

Without winds of grace, we're easily motivated by ill winds—the winds of legalism. Greed, fear, and guilt. The winds of popular opinion. When we're guided by the freeing winds of grace, however, we're more likely to make good choices—not out of guilt or greed or legalism but out of gratitude. Gratitude for the grace God showed us when He sacrificed His Son so "whoever believes in Him should not perish but have everlasting life" (John 3:16 NKJV).

The material world of old man Potter works another way. It says, *If your net worth is this much, you have arrived. If you use this product, you will be popular. If you live in this neighborhood, you are somebody. If you win this award, your worth is validated.* The material world demands that you *do* something to earn favor, often something underhanded, as in the case of Potter.

God doesn't work this way. His grace is a gift. There's nothing we can do to make God love us more. There's nothing we can do—or have done—to make God love us less. And when we accept this—not just nonchalantly agree that it's true but hide it in our very hearts—it fills us with the same kind of wonder that fills George as he races home in the snow late on that Christmas Eve. Full of joy, he realizes he had once been lost but now is found.

The author describes continuity errors, imperfections, and anachronisms within the film. How does God deal with errors and imperfections in the lives of the people who love Him?

_____

_____

_____

_____

Unconditional love is a wonderful gift from God. What are some innovative ways we can share this powerful gift with others?

_____

_____

_____

The Essence of Life Is Relationships

George, I'm an old man, and most people
hate me. But I don't like them either.
—OLD MAN POTTER

Poor Mr. Potter. He's Scrooge without the dream scenes. He is, depending on the source, a "hard-skulled character" (Peter Bailey), a "scurvy little spider" (George Bailey), and the "meanest man in the county" (Joseph the Angel, who also calls him the richest man in the county, but only, of course, in a materialistic sense). And the whole point of the movie, in the end, is that the essence of life is relationships, not money.

There's nothing new about that idea. In Matthew 22, a Pharisee who is an expert in the law asks Jesus which is the greatest commandment. Jesus replies, "'Love the Lord your God with all your heart and with all your soul and with all your mind.' This is the first and greatest commandment. And the second is like it: 'Love your neighbor as yourself.' All the Law and the Prophets hang on these two commandments" (vv. 35–40).

In other words, what matters most in life isn't having money and things but enjoying relationships with people and God. That's our purpose. What we're called to do. Which is why Potter is such a lonely man. Because he doesn't get it. He lives with the same meaninglessness as a cat chasing its tail.

The newspaper where I work recently asked readers to explain the meaning of life. The answers were diverse, but most were tinted with a clear sense of futility. "Many years ago, back in my college days when I was young and idealistic, I had all sorts of thoughts about the meaning of life, and it was really a big issue to me," wrote one person. "Over the years, I have decided there really is no meaning. We're just here."

Having personally survived Nazi death camps, Viktor Frankl studied what it was that allows some people to retain their humanity in inhumane circumstances. He found that it went beyond intellect or psychology. It came down to *meaning*—the ability to find purpose in what we do, no matter how seemingly insignificant the task might be.

"Being human," Frankl wrote in *Man's Search for Meaning*, "always points, and is directed, to something, or someone, other than oneself."

Indeed, when we try to fill our emptiness with something other than what was intended—riches instead of relationships—we're doomed. "People who want to get rich," wrote the apostle Paul to Timothy, "fall into temptation and a trap and into many foolish and harmful desires that plunge men into ruin and destruction. For the love of money is a root of all kinds of evil. Some people, eager for money, have wandered from the faith and pierced themselves with many griefs" (1 Timothy 6:9–10).

Russian author Leo Tolstoy told the story of a peasant who is offered all the land he could walk around in a day. The man hurries to get around as much as possible, his exertion so great he falls dead just as he gets back to where he had begun.

At the end of *It's a Wonderful Life*, isn't that the fate of old man Potter? He winds up with nothing. And George, though he had to be humbled to learn the lesson, winds up with everything. Not because of that basket of money. The reason George winds up with everything is that he realizes, more clearly than ever, where true riches lie: not in money or things, but in relationships.

Materialism is a constant threat and temptation not only at Christmastime but year-round. How does God help us combat the allure of materialism?

_____

_____

_____

_____

The film argues that relationships are more valuable than riches. Who are the people who have enriched your life beyond measure? Take a brief moment to thank God for them.

_____

_____

_____

LESSON 33

What Triggers True Change Is True Humility

Help me, Clarence. Get me back . . .
Please, God, let me live again.
—GEORGE, AFTER RETURNING TO THE PRESENT

You could say that lots of things led to George Bailey's redemption: The visit from Clarence. The answers to people's prayers. The love of a wife. The big hearts of the people of Bedford Falls. But at the core of his end-of-movie turnaround, the key to his "new life" is his own humility, his willingness to finally accept the truth of what Clarence has shown him. Without such humility, the other factors would have bounced off George without effect.

But, oh, George does not come easily to that point of view, does he? Face it: he's skeptical about Clarence from the moment the two first interact in the tollhouse on the bridge. He questions who Clarence is and what his motives are.

"What are you, a mind reader or something?" he says. "Who are you?"

He begins rationalizing that Clarence couldn't possibly be who he says he is.

"Oh, brother," he says. "I wonder what Martini put in those drinks?"

He laughs Clarence off as a joke. "You look about like the kind of an angel I'd get. Sort of a fallen angel, aren't you?"

More rationalization: "This is some sort of a funny dream I'm having here."

Then, the first hint of anger, which manifests itself as blame. After George asks to go home and Clarence points out he has no home, George says, "Now shut up! Cut it out! You're . . . you're . . . you're crazy! That's what I think . . . you're screwy, and you're driving me crazy too!"

He runs away, fleeing Bert and Ernie after his visit to the Granville house.

More rationalization, more pride-fueled insistence that he can get out of this jam on his own. "You've got me in some kind of a spell, or something. Well, I'm going to get out of it. I'll get out of it."

More defiance of Clarence and his authority. "That's a lie!" he says when Clarence tells him Harry died as a little boy after falling through the ice.

More anger: in the cemetery, George grabs Clarence by his overcoat lapels and, when told what's become of Mary, shoves him down, albeit without much oomph.

Then, finally, comes a subtle moment in the movie that, when you think about it, suggests George's ultimate change of heart. After confronting Mary, who, of course, doesn't recognize the man, he chases her downtown. A crowd gathers. He screams at her, desperately wanting her to recognize him. He grabs her. She flees. The crowd restrains George. "He needs a straitjacket!" says a man. The siren from Bert's police car wails.

That's when it happens. In his desperation—and only moments before he'll punch Bert—George cries out, "Clarence! Clarence! Where are you?"

For the first time, he's not rationalizing away the angel or running from him. He's seeking him. Running not from him, but *to* him.

He's running *from* the people who he earlier thought could corroborate his story and disprove Clarence, those he thought he could trust. And running *to* the bridge, the metaphorical symbol that spans life's troubled waters, the abyss between man and God.

Why does George come here? Because, for the first time, he trusts Clarence. Because this is where he first met him, he's hoping this is where he can find him again. Heaven knows—literally, Franklin and Joseph undoubtedly watching the action play out—his plans to disprove the silly angel have failed. His mother has shut the door in his face. His wife acts as if she doesn't know him. The people of Bedford Falls—or what Bedford Falls was before it became Pottersville—have turned on him. Heck, Bert, one of his best friends—or so he thought—is shooting at him, and based on the six pistol reports, these aren't warning shots.

In that moment, George is at the deepest depth of loneliness and betrayal. In his mind, he has nothing. He has nobody. He is, for the first time, truly broken. And so he runs to the one he now believes in: a silly angel.

"Clarence! Clarence! Help me, Clarence. Get me back. Get me back. I don't care what happens to me. Only get me back to my wife and kids. Help me, Clarence, please! Please! I want to live again!"

He is in utter anguish, leaning on the snow-covered bridge railing, burying his face in fists clenched with the frustration of being betrayed, empty, utterly alone.

"I want to live again," he cries. "Please, God, let me live again."

It's as if George is finally trusting Clarence and—suggests that final line—the One who sent the angel: God. As if he's finally willing to let this unlikely savior save him. As if he's finally dying to himself. "I don't care what happens to me," he says. He just wants to live again.

And in some ways, to live for the first time. Because when the snow begins falling again . . . when a friendly Bert shows up to help and not hurt him . . . when his lip starts bleeding . . . and when he discovers Zuzu's petals back in his pocket, the circumstances of his life, in that moment, are absolutely unchanged. What's changed, however, is his heart. George Bailey is a new man who sees with new eyes. And what triggered that change was his utter brokenness. Humility. His willingness, on that bridge, to give up relying on himself and to rely on something—someone—more trustworthy.

"Blessed are the poor in spirit," says Matthew 5, "for theirs is the kingdom of heaven. Blessed are those who mourn, for they will be comforted. Blessed are the meek, for they will inherit the earth. Blessed are those who hunger and thirst for righteousness, for they will be filled. Blessed are the merciful, for they will be shown mercy. Blessed are the pure in heart, for they will see God" (vv. 3–8).

They will, as a humbled George Bailey soon will, discover the truth: that it is, indeed, a wonderful life.

George Bailey does not arrive so easily to the truth that he has touched the lives of many. Why are we humans so resistant to the truth? Why does being confronted with the truth sometimes make us angry?

_____

_____

_____

_____

Read Matthew 5:1–12. What truths does the Sermon on the Mount reveal about humility?

_____

_____

_____

Fame Doesn't Equal Success, Nor Obscurity Failure

. . . 4-F on account of his ear, George fought the
battle of Bedford Falls . . . Air-raid Warden . . .
paper drives . . . scrap drives . . . rubber drives . . .
—JOSEPH, DESCRIBING GEORGE'S MUNDANE
ROLES DURING THE WAR

George Bailey longs to live an extraordinary life but winds up living an ordinary life—or so he believes. Sam Wainwright goes off to New York to make his fortune. Harry goes off to war and wins the Medal of Honor. Others go off to boldly serve their country. And yet George stays home to fight "the battle of Bedford Falls."

Our culture places a premium on adventure, doesn't it? We make movies and write books about people who go off to do daring things, not about people who stay home. Even if those who stay home live exemplary lives, we still tend to write them off as ho-hummers who never did anything particularly important.

Our culture places a premium on work, not on relationships. Think about it. When we meet someone, our first question isn't "So, what kind of positive impact are you having on the people around you?" No, it's "What do you do for a living?" It's not "How are you investing in others?" Instead, even if unspoken, it's "How much money do you make?" Our identity lies in jobs, titles, incomes, not in our connections to people.

But *It's a Wonderful Life* dares to spit in the eye of fame and fortune. It dares to say, "No man is a failure who has friends." It dares to say an ordinary guy, at least on the surface, may actually be an extraordinary guy. It dares to snub the value system of status quo and to exalt the value system of day-to-day goodness.

In so doing, it hammers home the wisdom of author and Bible teacher Oswald Chambers, who wrote: "We have to be exceptional in the ordinary things." And: "No man is born either naturally or supernaturally with character, he has to make character. Nor are we born with habits; we have to form habits on the basis of the new life God has put into us. We are not meant to be illuminated versions, but the common stuff of ordinary life exhibiting the marvel of the grace of God."[1]

Isn't that what George Bailey is all about? Isn't he about the common stuff of ordinary life exhibiting the marvel of the grace of God? The behind-the-scenes giving? The loaning of money to Violet? The using of his and Mary's honeymoon money to save the Building and Loan? The extending of loans to people whom Potter wouldn't trust?

"The great hindrance in spiritual life," wrote Chambers in *My Utmost for His Highest*, "is that we will look for big things to do. 'Jesus took a towel . . . and began to wash the disciples' feet.' There are times when there is no illumination and no thrill, but just the daily round, the common task. Routine is God's way of saving us between our times of inspiration. Do not expect God always to give you His thrilling minutes, but learn to live in the domain of drudgery by the power of God."[2]

Even if he longed for more, this is the life that George Bailey lived: Common. Routine. Touched, it would seem, by drudgery; he inherits the job, after all, that he told his father would drive him crazy, "this business of nickels and dimes and spending all your life trying to figure out how to save three cents on a length of pipe. I want to do something big and something important."

But the movie's conclusion suggests that George has spent his entire life doing things that *were* big and important; he just didn't realize it because he has bought into the world's value system of mountaintop living.

"We are not built for the mountains and the dawns and aesthetic affinities, those are for moments of inspiration, that is all," wrote

Chambers. "We are built for the valley, for the ordinary stuff we are in, and that is where we have to prove our mettle."[3]

It may sound as if to embrace such thinking requires a defeatist attitude. On the contrary: the suggestion isn't that we shouldn't dream big or aspire to greatness. The suggestion is that dreams and greatness often lie right where we live our lives, in the "routine" relationships at home, in our Bedford Falls worlds and not necessarily beyond.

Actor Richard Speight Jr., who played in the ten-part miniseries *Band of Brothers*, had the courage to put Hollywood in perspective. In an August 7, 2007, interview with ActorsLife.com, he was asked if he felt "successful."

That is a loaded question. I have a wipe-away board with four words on it: Steve, Jaci [his wife], This House. I wrote that so that any time I am frustrated because I didn't get the series I wanted or I have a big audition to prepare for or I don't have many lines [in] the episode I'm about to shoot, I can look at the board and remind myself that I have achieved so much in life. When you're on your deathbed, you're not going to think about the *In Style* party you got to go to or the sitcom you worked on.

The acting industry is like the hottest chick in your high school—no matter how much you love her and how hard you try to win her heart, she's never going to [care] whether you come or go. The sooner you can realize that, the better off you are.[4]

For George Bailey to accept that line of thinking isn't defeatist at all. In fact, it's that realization, after his interaction with Clarence the Angel, that brings "the obscure George" to full fruition as a human being. That makes him laugh in the face of his own struggles. That helps him see, for the first time, the wonder of the ordinary.

One might think "extraordinary" means *especially* ordinary, but it actually means *beyond* ordinary. How does God use ordinary people and circumstances to achieve extraordinary things?

_____

_____

_____

_____

Both the film and Scripture have a lot to say about friendship. Look up John 15:12–13, then think of the friends who have enriched your life. List them here and offer up prayers of gratitude to the Lord.

_____

_____

_____

LESSON 35

Bitterness Backfires on the One Who's Bitter

Frustrated and sick.

—Peter Bailey's description of Potter

Who knows why? Perhaps Henry F. Potter never saw selflessness modeled when growing up. Perhaps nothing he did was ever good enough for his father. Maybe he held a grudge against God because of a malady that rendered him unable to use his legs. But for whatever reason, Potter is a bitter man. "Frustrated and sick," Peter Bailey describes the man to his son George. "Sick in his mind, sick in his soul, if he has one."

And what does such bitterness do for Potter? Makes him forever crave what he doesn't already have. Bitterness is self-induced misery. When we vent our frustration at others, it only increases our own frustration. When we fail to forgive—in other words, free others to be human—we enslave ourselves. When we obsess over having what others have, we become all the poorer for doing so.

Think about it. Potter doesn't appear to have a single positive relationship. He despises the Baileys because they've won the respect of the community with their hearts, which is especially galling for a man who doesn't have much of one. He looks down on the poor, on those in the minority—he refers to George as being "trapped into frittering his life away playing nursemaid to a lot of garlic-eaters"—and, as Peter Bailey says, he looks down on "everybody that has anything that he can't have." He doesn't even seem to like or appreciate his own employees.

And where does it get him in the end? If George is feted as the richest man in town, Potter must be the poorest. If, in the words of Clarence, "no man is a failure who has friends," then isn't the friendless Potter a complete failure? If George's success is the warmth of family and friends who appreciate his bigheartedness, isn't Potter's failure his lack thereof?

To Potter, life is about amassing more, controlling more, having power. But in the end, where does such a value system get him? He may well be the loneliest person in Bedford Falls.

He is the antithesis of Philippians 2:3: "Do nothing out of selfish ambition or vain conceit, but in humility consider others better than yourselves." Potter does everything out of selfish ambition and vain conceit and considers nobody—God included, we can assume—better than himself. To which you want to say: "So, how's that working for you, Henry?"

If there's one thing separating George Bailey from Henry F. Potter, it's pride. George swallows his. Henry tethers himself to his pride like an anchor, where it drags him deep into the depths of despair.

Confronted by Clarence the Angel and challenged to look at his life differently, George—though not without resistance—ultimately casts aside his pride and looks at life differently. But Potter clings to his pride at all costs and, in the end, it spells his doom.

In *A Christmas Carol*, Scrooge, with the help of three ghosts, looks at his life differently and changes his approach to living it. Why? He casts aside his pride, which gives him, for the first time, new vision. Clarity. And though it's to others that he turns his attention for the first time, he ultimately benefits from this new vision.

It's a Wonderful Life director Frank Capra toyed with an ending that put Potter on the doorstep of the Bailey home late on that Christmas Eve, apparently prepared to return the eight thousand dollars he had kept from the Baileys. "Something," says the script, "tells him he is unworthy to be with those inside."[1]

And yet in God's economy, here's the good news: we're all welcome inside, regardless if we've lived a Potteresque life of selfishness. The question is, do we have the humility, as did Scrooge, to turn from our pasts? Do we have the courage to knock? Do we have faith in something beyond ourselves?

"Ask and it will be given to you," says Matthew 7:7. "Seek and you will find; knock and the door will be opened to you."

If only Henry F. Potter had done so, he would have learned what richness is really about. Instead, his pride drowned him in a poverty that all the money in the world couldn't save him from: his own bitterness.

The author defines bitterness as "self-induced misery." Have you ever been bitter about a certain situation and how you were treated? How did God help you release your bitterness?

_____

_____

_____

_____

The old saying "Pride cometh before a fall" is actually modified from Proverbs 16:18. Why is pride so harmful to our interactions and relationships with others?

_____

_____

_____

Living Simply Helps Us Appreciate What's Most Significant

Nobody ever changes around here. You know that.
—Uncle Billy to Harry after his nephew says, at the
train station, "Uncle Billy, you haven't changed a bit."

Author Henry David Thoreau may have said it, but Bedford Falls lived it. Thoreau encouraged people to "simplify, simplify." He wrote, "Give me that poverty that knows true wealth." He went into the woods at Walden Pond for two years and lived in a cabin roughly the size of your roadside java hut. (Never mind that he routinely went home to Concord to have his mother do his laundry.)

Thoreau believed that reducing your worldly footprint helps

you focus on truth and beauty. Living an uncluttered life increases your gratefulness for what you have. And untethering yourself from the weight of material belongings, financial demands, and time constraints brings a certain freedom.

Thoreau would have loved Bedford Falls. It was a place given to "simplicity, simplicity." If it didn't exude the bare-bones existence he experimented with on Walden Pond, there's not much, beyond old man Potter, to suggest it was a place wrapped in the trappings of materialism. It wasn't a place trying to impress itself, and others, with the glitz of style over substance. (Except, of course, Violet. "Why, this old thing? I only wear it when I don't care how I look.") Or a place where folks weren't forever trying to reinvent themselves while in desperate pursuit of the latest trend or fad or "answer."

"Uncle Billy," says Harry when stepping off the train, "you haven't changed a bit."

"Nobody ever changes around here," Billy answers. "You know that."

Now, fast-trackers may see that as a fault, the town's contentedness with the way it is. But I'd argue that that is a strength, a quiet contentment with what it is, an understated acceptance of its place in the world, an unpretentious security in the things that matter.

So, what matters in Bedford Falls? People matter. Relationships. The common good. When George tries to buy a suitcase for a planned trip overseas, he learns that Mr. Gower the druggist has already bought one for him and had his initials put on it. When he reluctantly goes to visit Mary, couples are enjoying the simplicity of evening walks. (In fact, in the short time the film shows George in front of the Hatch house, nearly twenty people walk by. Bedford Falls citizens may believe in Thoreau's simplicity, but they're clearly not the hermit he was.) Sure, Bedford Falls has a few me-first folks, such as Tom, who, despite desperate times during the run on the bank, insists on getting his full "two hundred and forty-two dollars" from the Building and Loan. But Ed, who has three hundred available, settles for twenty. And, of course, Mrs. Davis settles for a mere "seventeen fifty." (An amount, by the way, which she spoke out of the blue, George's grateful kiss in response equally unscripted.)

But for the most part the folks of Bedford Falls don't worship money and things. Mr. Martini and Nick could have kept serving George at the bar that Christmas Eve, but the higher value was George's well-being. "Why you drink so much, my friend?" asks Mr. Martini. "Want someone to take you home?" asks Nick.

With the exception of Sam Wainwright, even Bedford Falls folks who leave the simplicity of the town—when Mary goes off to college, for example—or attempt to leave—Violet and George—wind up appreciating its homespun virtues in the end. Mary may have the purest set of down-home values of them all; she returns to the place not only because of George but because she loves the place itself, including, of course, the Granville House. Violet, apparently inspired by the fund-raising effort for George, decides against New York, in part, we can assume, because she realizes the goodness of the place.

And George, as much as he'd have loved to travel the world, discovers on that Christmas Eve that contentedness isn't about building things or going places; it's simpler than that. It's about people, the very infrastructure on which Bedford Falls is built.

In the life-without-George sequence, Clarence introduces George to a Bedford Falls spoiled by a mindset of greed, speed, and complexity—the Potter influence, of course. People are gruff, out for themselves, and fixated on cheap thrills ("girls, girls, girls") and the mighty dollar. That Bedford Falls retains its simple, good self with George around suggests not only that we can be beneficiaries of such homespun goodness but that our very presence can help create it.

Christmas is a good time not only to remember the value of *people* but also the goodness of *place*. Think of a location important to your life and list the reasons you treasure it.

_____

_____

_____

_____

Society constantly pressures us to keep up with the latest trend, fad, technology, or celebrity. How do these things get in the way of what really matters in our lives and our faith?

_____

_____

_____

High Ideals Are an Honorable Pursuit

In my book he died a much richer
man than you'll ever be!
—GEORGE BAILEY, TO POTTER, REGARDING
HIS FATHER, PETER BAILEY

In his postmortem put-downs of Peter Bailey, Henry F. Potter derides the man as a failure whose impassioned protection of the little guy has imperiled Bedford Falls. "Peter Bailey was not a businessman," says Potter. "That's what killed him. Oh, I don't mean any disrespect to him, God rest his soul. He was a man of high ideals, so-called, but ideals without common sense can ruin this town." He then goes on to question loans Peter Bailey made to such folks as Ernie the cab driver and Mr. Martini.

Frankly, we don't know all that much about Peter Bailey. Perhaps some of what Potter suggests is true; after all, George himself admits his father was no businessman. And yet George respects his father so much that he winds up sacrificing his dreams to stay home, run the Building and Loan, and, in so doing, preserve the man's honor.

In George's defense of his father, the two warring factions aren't the "ideals" and "common sense" that Potter pits against each other. The two concepts at odds are living with heart or living without heart. Even if he doesn't specifically address Potter's no-common-sense allegation, George suggests that, yeah, maybe his father did lack a little in that department. Even if he doesn't say so, perhaps George knows that his father's kindheartedness got him burned from time to time by people he trusted who didn't make good on their payments. But he argues that the higher value here isn't common sense; it's ideals. Aspiring to help others. The character to see beyond one's self.

"Why, in the twenty-five years since he and Uncle Billy started this thing, he never once thought of himself," he says. "He didn't save enough money to send Harry to school, let alone me. But he did help a few people get out of your slums, Mr. Potter. And what's wrong with that?" Doesn't that generosity make people better citizens, better customers? George asks.

For the Baileys, the bottom line is people. For Potter, it's profit. And Henry F. Potter is absolutely right when suggesting that "ideals"—it's likely too painful for him to use the word *generosity*—can sometimes cut down on the financial bottom line. But George argues that there are things more valuable than bottom lines: Integrity. People. And giving them an opportunity to succeed.

As a newspaper columnist, I once did a series of stories about whether we should give handouts to people on street corners. What surprised me was how so many opinions about being taken advantage of by the homeless—"Is he really a vet? Couldn't he get a job? What if he spends it on booze?"—came from readers who identified themselves as Christians.

Really? The highest value here is *your* not getting exploited over a couple of bucks you might have given to someone? No, the highest value is helping the poor. Giving comes with certain risks; without a doubt, if you give money to the poor, you will, at times, be taken advantage of. You will give money to people who aren't, perhaps, as bad off as they suggest, or who may spend it on things you wouldn't want them to spend it on.

That's the small risk you take when daring to care for others. The good Samaritan had tons of reasons not to help the man who'd been beaten and left for dead; foremost, he was from a rival ethnic group. But he stopped and helped. Potter would have chastised him as a man of high ideals and no common sense. But in God's economy, he is honored. After all, Jesus healed people, brought people back to life, created food on the spot for people—without demanding background checks of those to whom He was giving.

The point isn't that we should frivolously give away money without thought. The point is that ideals do trump common sense. Heart trumps head. And, like Peter Bailey, we will all die richer when our lives have been lived with that in mind.

Charitable giving often increases during the Christmas season. Do people give out of guilt or genuine concern for others? If the end result is the same, why is one motivation better than the other?

_____

_____

_____

_____

Take time to read the parable of the good Samaritan (Luke 10:25–37). What does this passage teach us about givers? About recipients?

_____

_____

_____

LESSON 38

Lost Dreams Can Be Found Opportunities

Wish I had a million dollars . . . Hot dog!
—George, while trying the old-fashioned
cigar lighter at Gower's drugstore

Let's take this scene and consider what might have happened had George really gotten his wish. This, of course, isn't the first time he's slapped the cigar lighter at Gower's Drugs while wishing for a million bucks. He did so in the movie's second scene, when he arrives to work at the soda fountain as a boy. So, it's fair to say that, like a lot of us, George had dreams of wealth and travel and doing big, important things.

In fact, as he walks into Mr. Gower's drugstore as a young man, he's primed to live out that dream. He's just come from the luggage store, where he's been given a suitcase bought for him by Mr. Gower. He's leaving soon, he says, for Italy, Baghdad, and Samarkand, some pretty exotic places. (Samarkand is a city in present-day Uzbekistan, about 150 miles north of Afghanistan, and known as "the Rome of the East.")

His plans, however, all get derailed. That night, as George is returning from the dance with Mary, his father dies. And before long, George is stuck in Bedford Falls running his father's company.

But just for argument's sake, let's say George's cigar-lighter dream came true, and he suddenly had a million bucks in his wallet—nine $100,000 bills, nine $10,000 bills, nine $1,000 bills, and ten $100 bills. It's pure conjecture about how his life would have been different, but let's take our best shot.

For starters, George wouldn't have wound up at the high school dance that evening. Naw, when you have a million bucks in your back pocket, going to a high school dance would seem far beneath you. He may have gone downtown. He may have stayed in his room, counting his good fortune. But he wouldn't have gone to the dance; thus, he wouldn't have danced with Mary, nor married her.

After his father's death, he may have taken over the Building and Loan to satisfy the board of directors' wishes. But he had a million dollars; certainly, he could infuse the company with some of the money and hire an outsider to keep tabs on the forgetful Uncle Billy and the company. That would have freed him up for travel. But the outsider probably wouldn't have had a true Bailey heart, so Martini probably would have been turned down for a loan. Martini's heart would have hardened, and instead of running a friendly bar, he would have served "hard drinks . . . for men who wanna get drunk fast." And the company may have called in Ernie the cab driver's loan if he were late on a few payments, against Uncle Billy's protest. Desperate to make his loan payment and not disappoint his family, Ernie would have turned to a small-time life of crime involving door-to-door sales scams.

When the run on the bank exploded, George would have been sipping exotic wines in Samarkand. No way, given 1930s telegrams, the remoteness of Samarkand, and Potter's threat that "if you close your doors before 6 P.M. you will never reopen," would George have been able to bail out the Building and Loan in time. Desperate, his appointee as president may well have taken Potter's fifty-cents-on-the-dollar offer, and the sordid roots of Pottersville would have started growing.

As Clarence suggested in his life-without-George journey, with Potter in control, Bedford Falls would have taken on a dark, greedy edge. When George returned from his trip—who knows?—maybe he would have invested some of his money with Sam Wainwright and felt a certain obligation to date some of the women Sam introduced him to, and wound up marrying one of them and settling in New York to build bridges and airports and the like.

But what would have become of Bedford Falls?

Fortunately, as the Rolling Stones song reminds us, we can't always get what we want, but every once in a while, if we try, we might get what we need.

What George needed was Mary and the Bailey Building and Loan and Bedford Falls, and what Mary and Bailey Building and Loan and Bedford Falls needed was George. So let's be thankful his million-dollar dream didn't come true. Because though George certainly would have left his mark on the world—and probably an honorable one too—his not being where he truly belonged would have, as Clarence said about life without him, "left an awful hole."

Imagine suddenly becoming wealthy beyond your wildest dreams. Would you be happier? Why or why not?

_____

_____

_____

_____

It's hard to fathom the vast ripple effect a person's life has on others. Briefly consider your loved ones not being here. What are some ways you can show gratitude to them this week?

_____

_____

_____

LESSON 39

All That Glitters Is Not Gold

*Oh, yes, George Bailey. Whose ship has just come
in—providing he has brains enough to climb aboard.*
—Mr. Potter

When old man Potter offers George a job with his firm, it is a defining moment for the young Mr. Bailey. Remember the context: It is right after the Martini-house-dedication scene, which ends with George and Mary turning down an offer to join Sam Wainwright and his wife on a spontaneous jaunt down to Florida. They watch wistfully as Sam and his mink-and-jewel-clad wife ride off in their chauffeur-driven car. In a sense, it's another loss for George, the third time he's passed up an opportunity to leave Bedford Falls, even if this would have been only a short-term trip. As the couple walks back to the beaten-up Bailey car—interestingly, even Mary, the stoic, stay-at-home wife, seems touched by regret—a frustrated George kicks the driver-side door shut.

So, in the next scene, when George takes a puff on the cigar offered to him in Potter's office and starts hearing the old man's proposition, it truly is as if his ship has come in. Potter is offering George more than a job with his firm. He's extending him an opportunity to fulfill his latent dreams of travel and adventure. He's promising him twenty thousand dollars a year, nearly ten times what he's making now. He's offering him, in essence, a makeup call to at least get out and travel, if not leave Bedford Falls permanently. To explore the world. To be the man he always wanted to be.

Potter describes George, to his face, as "a young man who's been dying to get out on his own ever since he was born . . . a young man who has to sit by and watch his friends go places, because he's trapped . . . frittering his life away playing nursemaid to a lot of garlic-eaters." Though George wouldn't have approved of the anti-Italian racial slur at the end, it's clear that Potter has touched the young man's Achilles' heel, his latent regret that he's given up his dreams.

This, of course, is like the devil tempting Jesus. He knew that after forty days in the wilderness, Jesus was hungry, so he offered Him a quick solution to His hunger. In the same way, Potter knew George was hungry to live out his "do-important-stuff" dreams and offered him a quick solution to *his* hunger.

And George is poised to say yes. Though, of course, he wants

Mary to sign off on the deal, he realizes, as Potter says, that his ship has come in and he's prepared to leap aboard. But then comes the handshake. For George, Potter's touch—the script says "Potter's hand feels like a cold mackerel"—is like selling his soul to the devil. A wakeup call. A realization that though your head sometimes says one thing—"Take the job; you deserve it!"—you have to follow your heart, which often says something else.

George not only turns down the offer; he calls Potter a "scurvy little spider": "You spin your little webs and you think the whole world revolves around you and your money," he rants. "Well, it doesn't, Mr. Potter!"

What wins out, as it has before, is George Bailey's integrity. His unwillingness to put his desires above those of the community's. His unwillingness, in *Star Wars* terms, to go over to the dark side. And his ability to realize that not everything that glitters is gold.

Had George accepted Potter's offer, a sea change would have washed over Bedford Falls like a tsunami. As his employer, Potter would have pressured George to buy into his selfish value system; money, not people, would have been the bottom line, and Bedford Falls would have become the poorer for it. Meanwhile, though George may have traveled, pampered Mary, even fixed the newel post on the staircase, something new and more insidious than his go-places/do-things dreams would have begun eating him from the inside: the realization that he'd given up something all the gold in the world couldn't buy back—his personal integrity.

As it is, George seems to have asked himself the question from Mark 8:36—"What good is it for a man to gain the whole world, yet forfeit his soul?"—and had the courage to find the answer.

One definition of integrity is "the state of being undivided." In this sense, Mr. Potter and George are both undivided in their devotion to certain values. Who is the better person and why?

_____

_____

_____

_____

Have you ever pursued a dream for the wrong reasons? What kind of lessons did you learn or wisdom did you gain from the experience?

_____

_____

_____

LESSON 40

People Respond to Honorable Examples

Why don't you go to the riff-raff . . . and ask
them to let you have eight thousand dollars?
—MR. POTTER, TO GEORGE, AFTER THE MONEY GOES MISSING

Sometimes it takes a crisis for us to know who our true friends are and how deep those friendships go. When you think about it, *It's a Wonderful Life* isn't filled with affirmations about what a great guy everyone thinks George Bailey is. It's Harry who wins the Medal of Honor, while George does the volunteer grunt jobs back home. It's Sam who brings the new plastics-out-of-soybeans factory to Bedford Falls, even if it was George's idea. It's the Martinis' house dedication, even if it's George who made it happen. Meanwhile, George lives in the shadows, the wind beneath a lot of people's wings, but not the guy who everybody's celebrating.

Until, of course, that Christmas Eve when he's in trouble. Then, the measure of the man becomes clear. When George is seeking a loan to pay back the eight grand, Potter's sarcastic suggestion that he gather the money from the "riff-raff" in town becomes, ironically, the very answer to George's problem. Only George doesn't need to do the asking. Mary and others do it for him.

The lesson? People respond to those who inspire, which is what, in his quiet way, George does. All those "little things" he did to affirm others were not so little. The folks who had roofs over their heads because of the Baileys? They remembered. The brother who was free to go to college and go work for his new father-in-law? He remembered. The woman with the questionable reputation to whom George loaned money? She remembered. People notice givers, folks who put others first. People notice folks who take the high road. People whose lives are full of honorable examples.

The idea isn't that we should act a certain way to please people; that's a wrong motive. Said Paul in Galatians 1:10: "Am I now trying to win the approval of men, or of God?" We should act a certain way because that brings glory to God. That said, a lifetime of other-oriented living doesn't go unnoticed, even if we're not feted with thank-you banquets along the way.

It's been said that the measure of our lives is reflected in the number of people who will grieve our passing when that life is over. Or the number of people who will come to our rescue when we're in trouble. Certainly, George Bailey learned that lesson. On Christmas Eve, as he watches his friends step forward with their contributions to the "Help George" fund, he's clearly overwhelmed by the generosity.

What's happening, of course, is simple payback. A man who has given to others his entire life is finally getting the collective thank-you he's long deserved. Because people don't forget kindness.

Who inspires you? Jot down their names and consider ways you would like to thank them for their encouragement and inspiration.

The author writes that "people don't forget kindness." Who is your favorite character in the film who ends up on the receiving end of George's kindness. Why?

LESSON 41

Helping Others Requires Sacrifice

George saved his brother's life that day. But
he caught a bad cold which infected his left
ear. Cost him his hearing in that ear.
—Joseph the Angel

Even if it is more blessed to give than to receive, we can't ignore the fact that sacrificing for others often comes with a price. We might like to believe otherwise, but the truth is that giving can take its toll on us. It necessarily forces us to give up something of ourselves for the betterment of someone else.

Let's take George Bailey. He gave up his aspirations to go places and do things in order to focus on bettering his family, the family business, and Bedford Falls. He could have traveled. He could have gone to college. He could have built bridges and airports. But he gave it all up, even if somewhat unwillingly, for higher purposes.

In the 1980s, the idea that we could "have it all" took root in American culture, the idea that we could pursue, with equal passion, work, careers, family, faith, whatever.[1] And, really, the idea sounds inviting. Why couldn't we give endlessly to every aspect of our lives? Why shouldn't we?

Because, of course, we each have a limited supply of time, money, creativity, and energy. Something always has to give. And what we value deepest in our lives is what we devote ourselves to most earnestly.

Good families, for example, require submission of the individual to the collective interests of others. There's no other way it can be. When you marry, you either start practicing the art of self-denial—as you'd hope your mate would do—or you're destined for a lifetime of marital disharmony. Because relationships require sacrifice. When you start a family, that willingness to give of yourself necessarily increases because children require time, attention, money, creativity—all that stuff you once could hoard for yourself or for you and your spouse.

Look at missionaries, who do some of the most selfless work in the world. They willingly sacrifice the comforts of home, of familiarity, of social norms so they can serve others.

Consider people who serve in the military. They give up individualism and conform to standards not necessarily of their own choosing. Why? Because the collective whole is strengthened by the sacrifices of individuals.

Think about those who choose to follow Christ. It is easier and more comfortable not to enter into such a relationship because it requires risk, giving up control, allowing someone else to lead. "He must become greater," John 3:30 says; "I must become less."

Look at folks who build relationships with other people. Every time we take a step toward someone else, it means giving up something of ourselves. It may be time. Comfort. Money. Peace. But something. Because in stepping toward someone else, we're essentially agreeing to sacrifice our own needs for theirs.

Isn't that how George spends most of his life? Oh, sure, you could argue he had no other choice but to commit to Bedford Falls and not his dreams. Not so. Plenty of people, if told that the only way the board would preclude Potter from taking over the Building and Loan would be if they committed to being executive director themselves, would have said, "Thanks but no thanks. I'm off to college, even if I do look old enough to be a professor." But George stayed.

When, at the train station, Ruth mentions to George and Uncle Billy how her father wants new hubby Harry to work for her dad, the scene could have played out like this:

HARRY: Ruth spoke out of turn. I never said I'd take it.

You've been holding the bag here for four years,

and . . . well, I won't let you down, George.

GEORGE: You got that right, buster. I'm tired of being
everybody's go-to guy. What about me? What about
my dreams? What about *my* needs? While you were
off at college making All-American, I was back here
in Bedford Falls going crazy trying to figure out how
to save three cents on a length of pipe. I want to do
something big and something important. So, you'd
better not let me down. You can do research for
Ruth's father down the line. For now, you're the new
executive director of the Building and Loan. And good
luck trying to get Uncle Billy to remember his first
name.

But, of course, he didn't.

Likewise, it would have been more comfortable to ignore the
rush on the bank and take off on the honeymoon with Mary. "Ernie,
get us to the train station. And for an extra ten bucks, don't tell anyone we saw that Bedford Falls was on the verge of selling out to old
man Potter. It'll just be our little secret."

But, of course, he didn't.

Instead, George sacrificed his own dreams and aspirations for
the betterment of the whole. Just as he paid a price for saving Harry
in that icy pond—he lost the hearing in his left ear—he pays a price
for saving the town. But as the story plays out, the great news about
sacrifice is this: When we lose ourselves for others, we ultimately find
ourselves, don't we? When we let go of our selfish inclinations, we

live life at a deeper, fuller level than we could have ever imagined. When we dare to place others above ourselves—"If anyone has material possessions and sees his brother in need but has no pity on him, how can the love of God be in him?" (1 John 3:17)—we manifest the God of the universe to the world.

And that's one sweet surrender.

Think of a time when you made a sacrifice for the greater good of a certain cause or relationship. Was it worth it? Why or why not?

_____

_____

_____

_____

The prevalent American concept of "having it all" is hard to resist. How does relentlessly pursuing everything run counter to how God wants us to live our lives?

_____

_____

_____

LESSON 42

Look for Friends Who Bring Out the Best in You

Nice girl, Mary . . . [the] kind who will
help you find the answers, George.
—GEORGE'S MOTHER

We don't know a whole lot about Mrs. Bailey, George's mother. We first see her at the dinner before the graduation party, and frankly, she comes off as a bit of a worrywart. She's worried Harry's suit will get torn in her two sons' hyped-up, pre-dance commotion. Worried that George and Harry's food will get cold. Worried that Harry is taking her best Haviland plates for food to be served at Harry's dance. And, of course, there's her odd first reference to the two. "You two idiots!" But we like the woman much better after the scene in which George leaves the party for Harry and Ruth, and she encourages him to start seeing Mary Hatch.

We realize that she just wants what's best for George. Which, of course, is why she suggests he call on Mary, who's back in town after going off to college. George tells her that Mary's taken; Sam Wainwright is interested in her. But Mrs. Bailey persists. Sam is in New York, she says; you're here. In other words: home-court advantage, George. Besides, she points out—and here's where we start realizing she's a woman of deep insight—Sam is more interested in Mary than Mary is interested in Sam. No, it's George whom Mary favors. "Why, she lights up like a firefly whenever you're around," she tells her son.

Of all she says in this short exchange, perhaps the most insightful line is the one about how Mary is a nice girl, the "kind who will help you find the answers, George." It says two things about Mrs. Bailey. First, she's perceptive enough to know that George is questioning some things about his life, which is true. And second, she's perceptive enough to know that Mary would bring out the best in her son.

And she's absolutely right. Mary is the perfect fit for George, if he could just muster the courage to forget about Sam Wainwright—who, by the way, seems to have plenty of female companionship in the Big Apple—and pursue her. As the film unfolds, we realize that Mary is really something of a quiet hero.

For starters, she's smart. Despite her anger at George for being reluctant to pursue her—"What did you come here for?" she asks and, after he leaves, shatters her "Buffalo Gals" record—she turns on fake charm when Sam Wainwright calls, to tweak George's jealousy button. "That's awfully sweet of you, Sam . . ." And it works enough to get George at least back in the ball game, if not barking signals at the line of scrimmage. Speaking of smart, it's Mary who comes up with the idea to use their honeymoon money to save the Building and Loan.

Mary is not only smart but resourceful. She's one of those grow-where-you're-planted types. While George and relatives keep the Building and Loan alive on that rainy run-on-the-bank day, Mary spiffs up the Granville house for their honeymoon night. (Which raises a question: Did she somehow secretly buy the house before the wedding with the idea of surprising George? An earlier script has her buying it *during* the bank run, which seems a tad implausible given that it's probably a Saturday and she would have had to do all this in just over three hours, given that the bank run starts about 2:45 P.M., according to the office clock, and ends at 6 P.M., when the Building and Loan closes.)

Besides being smart and resourceful, Mary is loyal, so loyal that on that Christmas Eve when George goes ballistic, she sticks by him. Oh, sure, she tells him to leave—who can blame her after his violent behavior? But after he does so, what does she do? Something that harks back to Mrs. Bailey's line about how Mary is someone who'll help him find the answers. She prays for her husband. She encourages the whole town to pray for her husband. And, knowing Mary, she didn't browbeat anyone for money, just told them the truth about the missing eight thousand dollars.

Those prayers, of course—and George's own prayers—ultimately lead to the answer to the question George has wrestled with his whole life: Does my life really matter if I don't go off and do important stuff?

The lesson for us, of course, is to find friends—or encourage our children to find friends—who care enough to bring out the very best in us. Who won't drag us down but who will build us up. And, yes, who, as Mrs. Bailey so astutely observed, will help us find the answers. "A righteous man is cautious in friendship," says Proverbs 12:26, "but the way of the wicked leads them astray."

Look for Friends Who Bring Out the Best in You

Who in your life has "helped you find the answers," as Mrs. Bailey says? What are some ways you can show your gratitude and thank the Lord for their contribution to your faith journey?

_____

_____

_____

_____

The author refers to Mary Bailey as "one of those grow-where-you're-planted types." What does the parable of the sower (Matthew 13:1–9) reveal about stewardship, discernment, and our God-given talents?

_____

_____

_____

Desperation Can Be a Catalyst for Great Things

How much do you want?
—Freshly married Mary Bailey, offering
a roll of wedding-present cash to the
desperate Building and Loan customers

Desperate times, the saying goes, call for desperate measures. That may be true, but the more precise quotation might be: "Desperate times trigger imaginative solutions." Too often, when times get desperate, what do we do? We give up and panic. Remember the bank-run scene in *It's a Wonderful Life*? People are panicking. Giving up. But George calms them down. "Don't you see what's happening?

Potter isn't selling. Potter's buying! And why? Because we're panicky and he's not."

Talk about desperate. George has half the town clamoring for money and threatening to link hands with Potter. If he doesn't do something quickly, it's curtains for the Building and Loan, himself, Mary, and, more broadly, Bedford Falls. But Mary—ironically, who initially wanted to run away from this disaster—comes up with an eleventh-hour solution to save the day: the couple's honeymoon money, two thousand dollars' worth. Out of desperation comes a creative solution.

The Christmas Eve scene provides another wonder-out-of-woe example. George faces the ultimate desperation, the belief that his life has been such a failure that it's not worth going on. In fact, his so-called solution—he's contemplating suicide—is an example not of imaginative thinking based on desperation, but of *not* using desperation, like water through the turbines of a dam, to create a powerful, positive solution. We'll need to look to Mary for that. As George leaves the house, Mary, in her own desperation, turns to the two sources she knows can help: God and people. And, really, isn't it George's own desperation that leads him to pray?

People react to desperation in two ways. They allow it to stifle them, panic them, defeat them. Or they use it to inspire them, encourage them, lift them to new ways of thinking. When we take the initiative, the imagination starts flowing. And good things happen. In his book *Chesapeake*, James Michener wrote:

A ship, like a human being, moves best when it is slightly athwart the wind, when it has to keep its sails tight and attend its course. Ships, like men, do poorly when the wind is directly behind, pushing them sloppily on their way so that no care is required in steering or in the management of sails; the wind seems favorable, for it blows in the direction one is heading, but actually it is destructive because it induces a relaxation in tension and skill. What is needed is a wind slightly opposed to the ship, for then tension can be maintained, and juices can flow and ideas can germinate, for ships, like men, respond to challenge.[1]

When desperate times come, our initial response is often panic. What solution for desperation does Philippians 4:4–9 offer us?

_____

_____

_____

_____

Read Romans 8:28. Why does God often allow hardship to bring about positive change in us? Think of a time this happened to you. What did you learn?

_____

_____

_____

LESSON 44

Miracles Happen

George, it's a miracle! It's a miracle!
—MARY, AS SHE PREPARES FOR THE TOWNSPEOPLE
TO ARRIVE WITH THEIR "OFFERINGS"

The Scriptures are full of miracles. But I wonder if, even as believers in the One behind such miracles, we are doubting Thomases when it comes to miracles in our own times. Some might argue that we've cheapened miracles, ascribing supernatural causes to what, in the big picture, are fairly ordinary occurrences, say, the United States' "miracle on ice" in 1980, when the United States won the Gold Medal in Olympic ice hockey. Others, myself among them, would argue that perhaps the truth is quite the opposite. If not every amazing unfolding of events qualifies, maybe we overlook miracles right in front of us because our "qualifying standards" are so unreasonably high.

After all, wasn't it Isaac Newton who said, "In the absence of other proof, the thumb alone would convince me of God's existence"?

At any rate, Mary Bailey believes that a miracle is afoot on this snowy Christmas Eve. And, remember, when she mentions this aloud as she prepares the living room for the arrival of guests bearing gifts, she has no idea of the transformation that George has undergone. No idea of his scary but life-changing tour of Bedford Falls/Pottersville. No idea about Clarence's visit to her husband. Instead, she's referring to the town's reaction to the news that George is in trouble and needs help.

She leads George, who's carrying a couple of kids on his back, downstairs in front of the Christmas tree. With a single swoop of an arm—creative "preparation"—she clears off a couple of tables for the money basket and instructs George to stand right there. "George, it's a miracle! It's a miracle!"

At this point, George is too busy trying to kiss her—kind of a miracle in itself in that the last time they were together, a few hours before, he was lumbering through that same living room with all the anger of King Kong in Times Square—to really appreciate what was unfolding.

And then it happens. Uncle Billy arrives with the basket of money, trying, breathlessly, to explain what had happened (and perhaps secretly thrilled that the town's bigheartedness has pushed him off the hot seat with George!). But perhaps, like many of us, he's too practical to see the bigger picture.

"Mary did it, George! Mary did it! She told a few people you were in trouble, and they scattered all over town collecting money."

Mary knows better. This, she's already decided, is not just about people and dollars and big hearts. It's about something far more wondrous: a miracle.

And you have to believe that it wasn't the only miracle on this Christmas Eve. When everyone has left, when the kids go to sleep, when George tries to explain to Mary what happened to him, how else could he describe it? In the movie, George, of course, does little to explain how he once was lost but now is found, was blind but now he sees. Instead, you can see the miracle in his eyes. When, while on that snowy bridge, he realizes Bert knows him, his lip is bleeding, and Zuzu's petals are in his pocket. When he runs home in the snow, his heart so full of love that, amid all the pain he's been through, he even stops to offer Christmas greetings to old man Potter. When he wraps his wife and children in his arms and showers Mary with kisses.

Remember, at this point he has no idea of the redemption that's en route to the Bailey home, love dollars, respect, paid to a man who's given so much to others. All he knows is that he, too, has experienced a miracle that had nothing to do with changed circumstances and everything to do with perhaps the greatest miracle of all.

A changed heart.

A core message in both the Bible and *It's a Wonderful Life* is the powerful impact a changed heart has on the lives of others. How does George's transformation in the film reflect how God's grace and love work toward our salvation?

_____

_____

_____

_____

Miracles aren't limited to grand demonstrations, like walking on water or raising someone from the dead. Small miracles occur every day. What are some small miracles that have happened in your life this week?

_____

_____

_____

LESSON 45

Age Is Insignificant: How You Live Is Not

Aw, youth is wasted on the wrong people.
—MAN ON PORCH WHO THINKS GEORGE SHOULD KISS
MARY "INSTEAD OF TALKING HER TO DEATH"

George and Mary are walking home from the graduation dance when young Mr. Bailey literally promises her the moon. She heartily accepts. It's a sweet moment for the couple; however, it isn't for the crotchety old guy on his front porch who seems perturbed by something, perhaps their voices interrupting his reading of the evening paper.

"Why don't you kiss her instead of talking her to death?" he suggests with no particular politeness.

George considers the idea, but the man has no such patience. "Aw, youth is wasted on the wrong people," he mutters, then heads into his house.

Interesting hypothesis: youth is wasted on the wrong people.

We're not sure what the guy on the porch meant—nor are we sure why it appears he's wearing not one, but two undershirts—but his comment seems to have a touch of lament to it, as in: *If I were young again, I certainly wouldn't waste the opportunity that you are.*

Funny how so many young people desperately want to grow up and how many older people desperately want to grow "down"—go back to a younger age. What's wrong with being content where you are?

If *It's a Wonderful Life* doesn't overtly address themes of aging, it does so indirectly. In the end, one of the lessons George learns in his tour with Clarence is about finding contentment despite life's circumstances. It is the stuff of Philippians 4:11–13:

I have learned to be content whatever the circumstances. I know what it is to be in need, and I know what it is to have plenty. I have learned the secret of being content in any and every situation, whether well fed or hungry, whether living in plenty or in want. I can do everything through him who gives me strength.

Applied to aging, the concept is simple: be satisfied where you are. Age is not important; how you live, regardless of your age, is. A friend of my mother's husband died at eighty-five—while windsurfing in the Cook Islands. Meanwhile, I've taught a few twenty-one-year-old college students who seem already resigned to life as a meaningless wait for who-knows-what, their faces locked in that half-bored/half-angry expression of unhappy campers in a really long postal line.

If my math is correct, we each lose one day every twenty-four hours, the same rate for the eighty-year-old as for the forty-year-old and the twenty-year-old. It's like a reservoir being drawn down inches a day; the water level gets lower wherever you are on the lake. The only difference is that some of us have less water beneath us than others.

Which isn't to say that we need to be dead serious about aging. The most secure people I know, some in their seventies and eighties, laugh constantly about growing older. I think of a seventy-five-year-old woman who jokes about having been through half an alphabet of medical problems, but who lives with incredible zest.

So, don't pity people who turn sixty, seventy, or eighty. Pity those who can't find contentment with wherever they are in life. Those who miss the wonder of right now. Those who, whatever their ages, have turned bitter, like the two–T-shirt guy in the movie, and miss the joy of seeing two young people in love.

Sometimes the world feels rushed, fretful, and chaotic; our hectic lives are pulled in every direction. What are some ways this week you can take a breath and explore God's creation and the "wonder of right now"?

_____

_____

_____

_____

Why is contentment so hard to come by? Is contentment dependent on your age or mindset? What does the Bible reveal about contentment? Look to Psalm 37:3–4, Ecclesiastes 3:13, 1 Timothy 6:6–11, and Hebrews 13:5 for a good start.

_____

_____

_____

The Richest People in Town Might Have Little Money

A toast . . . to my big brother, George.
The richest man in town!
—Harry Bailey

Like the proverbial blind man and the elephant, people take away different messages from *It's a Wonderful Life*, depending on what part of the movie they "feel." Some might tell you it's about redemption; others, about faith; still others, about the goodness of small-town America. But it's fairly hard to miss the friendship theme embodied in Harry Bailey's toast at movie's end. For many, it puts the biggest lump in the throat, Harry Bailey having been flown through a snowstorm to support his brother.

Never mind that Harry, who's benefited from George's sacrifices numerous times over the years—and would likely have just cashed a nice back-pay check from the Army—doesn't plop even a quarter in the laundry-basket coffers. What he does with his toast is quiet the revelry long enough to distill his brother's life into two sentences. "A toast," he says, "to my big brother, George. The richest man in town."

Words worth their weight in gold. Words that summarize George Bailey's life. Words that undoubtedly humble his brother. Clarence underscores the theme with his words, written in the front of the book given to George, about how no man is a failure who has friends. And really, it's hard to argue that this is the movie's deepest theme. "This is what the picture is about," wrote Roger Rosenblatt in a December 11, 2000, essay in *Time* magazine, "the subtle and casual surprise of friendship."[1]

Interesting concept, friendship. It lacks the depth and breadth of our relationship with God, the romance and intrigue of our relationships with our mates, the emotional bonds of our relationships with our children. In some ways, friendship is the whir of the air conditioner in our workplace, quiet, in the background, yet essential to our well-being. It's the fire department, on call if there's an emergency. It's all the unspoken commitment to one another that only rarely is galvanized in such an overt, emotional way as the one Harry creates with his toast. And yet where would we be without it?

"The emotion," wrote Rosenblatt, "is generally undemonstrative; it is made up of the things we do *not* do—betray, belittle, be harsh. When it does manifest itself, we often don't see it coming, which is where friendship gets its power—from the slow, cordial dance of ordinary life."[2]

A cab driver. A cop. A forgetful uncle. The town flirt. A far-off boyhood pal, Sam Wainwright. George may have not thought much about how he was friends with each of these people, but in the end, he's reminded that not only is this the case but he's been integral to these people's lives.

We busy ourselves with the stuff of living: going to work, raising families, volunteering, serving at church, whatever. Amid it all, friendships can get lost. When my father died—I was forty-two at the time—I'll never forget standing in the church to offer a eulogy. I looked out at the sea of faces and, among some I didn't even recognize, there was a sprinkling of friends I hadn't seen in years. Friends I'd known since I was twelve. Friends who I'd never imagined would have taken the time to show up. And it comforted and encouraged me in a way that still moves me today.

It's as if we treat friendship with a certain ho-humness. Intellectually, George certainly understood its power—and long before his journey with Clarence. Remember when Potter is trying to take over the Building and Loan after Peter Bailey's death? George stands up for his father and his generosity—friendship with dollar bills attached—toward others. "People," he tells Potter, "were human beings to him, but to you, a warped, frustrated old man, they're cattle. Well, in my book he died a much richer man than you'll ever be!"

Interesting. Harry Bailey's toast was not the movie's first mention of how "richness" isn't about money or materialism but about people and how we treat them. That first mention came from George. But if he recognized it in his father and lived it out in his own life, George nevertheless had grown to take it for granted—until three reminders on Christmas Eve: Clarence showing George his influence on others, Mary gathering a roomful of his friends who came bearing—*ka-ching!*—gifts, and, of course, Harry hammering it all home with his toast.

Thus did he begin the evening feeling like the loneliest man in town—and wind up being honored as the richest man in town.

The Richest People in Town Might Have Little Money

What does it mean to be rich? Answer this question from an emotional or spiritual perspective, not in terms of material wealth.

_____

_____

_____

_____

Read about Jesus healing a paralyzed man (Mark 2:1–12). Although we may think of this story as one of faith, what does it reveal about the power of friendship?

_____

_____

_____

The World Needs More Sentimental Hogwash

Sentimental hogwash!
—Old Man Potter

Potter has no place in his world for sentiment. Greed doesn't mix well with the stuff. Thus, in the scene where George is defending Bedford Falls' need for the Building and Loan—"If only to have some place where people can come without crawling to Potter"—the crotchety old coot utters the two words "sentimental hogwash."

People who lack something in their lives rationalize their okayness by ridiculing that "something" in others. Without a doubt, the movie is heavily spiced with sentimentalism. But that bothers some people—those with perhaps a touch of Potter in them—and says more about them than about the movie.

On December 22, 2010, Pulitzer Prize–winning columnist Paul Greenberg confronted a critic of the movie with the same reasoning. In his newspaper column, syndicated by Tribune Media Services, Greenberg wrote of a college professor who had written that if the movie can be "an enriching Norman Rockwell experience, it also can be smothering, where you end up marrying the girl you went to high school with, and you never get to go to Europe. . . . It tells us George is one of the most sad and lonely and tragic characters ever imagined. I cry when I see it."[1]

Greenberg's response: "Me, I cry for the professor. To me, nothing in the movie seems as sad as the professor's analysis of it."[2]

George Bailey as tragic? "Come on," wrote Greenberg. "Why, he's the richest man in town, as his brother says at the end of the movie. He makes Mr. Potter, the stock plutocrat in the story, look like a pauper. That's because George Bailey has loved and sacrificed and built and given and stood alone a time or two. That is, he has lived. He has not gone through life as a tourist. Never getting to Europe does not strike me as the kind of experience that qualifies for tragedy."[3]

Those who find the movie laced with too much sentiment fail to realize that we live in a world with far too little of the stuff. Tender emotions are what connect us with the God who created us and those around us. They're what make us human. But too many people wall themselves away from them, à la Potter, and bravely pretend they're trivial, sentimental hogwash.

Deep down, though, it's what we long for: to love and to be loved. To care for others and to be cared for. To serve and to be served. It's what we were made for. Relationship. And, yes, it necessarily comes with heart tugs, some of joy, some of sorrow.

Without it we are dust. So, yes, bring on the sentimental hogwash. It's what reminds us we are, like the Baileys' living room on Christmas Eve—alive.

The world can be a cynical place, making it difficult to connect emotionally with others. What are some ways to reach across the divides that separate us and express God's love to others?

_____

_____

_____

_____

If we are created in God's image, what can we discern about God's emotions toward us? About our emotions toward Him?

_____

_____

_____

LESSON 48

Pay Attention to the Task at Hand

And did you put the envelope in your pocket?
—GEORGE

Yeah . . . yeah . . . maybe . . . maybe.
—UNCLE BILLY

Poor Uncle Billy. He's been having problems with forgetfulness since his midfifties—George's wedding, his age, you name it—and on Christmas Eve 1945 he's seventy-three. He should be retired and playing shuffleboard in Florida. But, God bless him, there he is, still giving his all for Bailey Building and Loan.

The problem is "his all" isn't always enough. All he has to do is deposit the eight thousand dollars in the bank, and yet he still manages to accidentally wrap the envelope inside a copy of the *Bedford Falls Sentinel* and leave it in Potter's lap. Uncle Billy's heart is in the right place; he got so busy boasting about Harry's Congressional Medal of Honor that he placed the deposit on his mind's back burner. And in Uncle Billy's case, that burner is way, way back.

Sometimes we get so busy thinking about things down the road that we forget about the important stuff happening right in front of us. That doesn't mean the answer, as Uncle Billy suggests, is to tie strings around our fingers or, the new-millennial equivalent, put reminders on our smart-phone calendars. The answer is to take life one task at a time and do each task well, instead of getting so far ahead of ourselves that we get behind.

It's really about priorities. "But seek first his kingdom and his righteousness," says Matthew 6, "and all these things will be given to you as well. Therefore do not worry about tomorrow, for tomorrow will worry about itself. Each day has enough trouble of its own" (vv. 33–34).

It's worth noting that George, when given a chance to blame Uncle Billy for misplacing the money, does not do so. Likewise, we should go easy on those who make mistakes because they are, as it were, "out to lunch." Meanwhile, we need to be reminded that small oversights can lead to big problems—a lesson that would have haunted Uncle Billy the rest of his life had not Mary and the community ridden to the rescue.

Pay Attention to the Task at Hand

Think of a time when you "gave your all," but it didn't seem like it was good enough. How did God comfort you during this difficult time?

_____

_____

_____

_____

Has your forgetfulness ever hurt someone who was depending on you? What did the situation reveal about forgiveness and grace?

_____

_____

_____

LESSON 49

People Can Change

George Bailey? What's he want?
—MARY'S IRASCIBLE MOTHER, MRS. HATCH, AFTER LEARNING
THAT GEORGE HAS DROPPED BY TO SEE HER DAUGHTER

We don't see much of Mary's mom, Mrs. Hatch, in the movie, but what we do see reminds us that she wouldn't be much fun if you got stuck sitting next to her at a dinner party.

So, what do we know about her? Well, either she's divorced or widowed, given the "Mrs. J. W. Hatch" we see on the mailbox before the pivotal scene when Mary invites George inside. We're thinking her husband is deceased, unless he is alive and didn't show up for his own daughter's wedding—or director Frank Capra just chose not to introduce him to us. Given that the Hatches live in a fairly nice,

Father Knows Best house, we'd also suggest that, if deceased, her husband left Mrs. Hatch fairly well off or, if the two are divorced, she did well in divorce court. Unless, of course, she has a great-paying job (which wasn't likely for a woman in that decade) or her well-heeled folks left a bundle of dough for her.

We know Mrs. Hatch helped raise at least two children: Mary and her little brother, Marty, who, you'll recall, first got George and Mary together at the high school dance. (And played a more prominent role in the opening sledding scene until a revised script did little more than show him as the second kid down the sled run on his shovel.)

So, if the woman is financially secure, if she lives in a comfortable house in a comfortable little town, and if she has managed to raise two first-rate children—Mary, of course, is top-notch, and Marty is clearly a great guy who, remember, helped capture the Bridge at Remagen in World War II—then why is she so darn crotchety?

In the scene where George visits Mary, she treats her daughter's friend as if he's a total loser, meanwhile ballyhooing the two-timing Sam Wainwright as the greatest thing since radio theater. "Don't you leave the house," she tells Mary—as if her daughter is eight years old—"Sam Waaaaaaaaiiiiiiiiiiinwright promised to call you from New York tonight."

Then she calls her daughter an idiot. Remember? When Mary tells George that Sam wants to talk to him on the phone, the nosy "mom-ster" says from upstairs, "He doesn't want to speak to

George, you idiot!" In fairness, it's true that George first referred to Mary as "brainless" in that soda fountain scene, but he was just a kid at the time, so has an excuse. As an adult, Mrs. Hatch should have known better. Finally, when George and Mary embrace, Mrs. Hatch turns and walks away with a pained look on her face as if she'd just seen the family cat squashed by a milk truck.

The second scene she's in is the brief post-wedding appearance where, if you watch closely, you'd swear she was at a funeral. She follows George and Mary down the steps, gets a quick kiss from Mary, then, next to George's mom, shakes her head with a look on her face that suggests either she's just eaten a tart pickle or her daughter has sold her soul to the devil. Didn't she realize what a catch George was? Apparently not.

Let's face it: Mrs. Hatch is a grumpy, bitter, glass-is-a-quarter-full type. Ah, but her final scene brings redemption. It's the money-collecting scene in George and Mary's living room, and we realize, for the first time, the woman knows how to smile. No, she doesn't say anything. No, we don't see her adding to the George Bailey Redemption Fund or even propping a grandkid or two into her arms, but she smiles. She laughs. You get the idea that she understands, perhaps for the first time, what a fine man her son-in-law actually is.

Had Mary had less faith in George, instead of praying for him and launching the fundraiser when he left the house that evening, she could have run to Mom's place and complained about what a rotten husband he was. Mrs. Hatch may have been more than happy to welcome her and the kids on a permanent or semipermanent basis, as it would have given her the quiet satisfaction that she was right about George being a loser and about Sam Wainwright being a far better choice.

Instead, though Capra doesn't play out her story, we're left to assume that somewhere between George and Mary's wedding day and that Christmas Eve—a thirteen-year span between 1932 and 1945—Mrs. Hatch's heart, like the Grinch's, grew in size.

Why? We're left to conjecture on that one. Perhaps the war years softened her. Remember, she joined George's mom to sew for the Red Cross and did flash a brief smile in that scene. Maybe the experience made her appreciate all she had, including an honorable son-in-law who wasn't having to march off to Anzio or Omaha Beach. Perhaps a sermon touched her heart. Or maybe she was bitter right up to that Christmas Eve, but seeing the outpouring of love for George melted her heart like Paul's on the road to Damascus.

At any rate, if Mrs. Hatch seemed miserable early in the movie, she ultimately learned to smile, laugh, and appreciate what she had in Bedford Falls. And, thus, she was able to feel the joy abounding in the Bailey living room on that Christmas Eve. A reminder to never underestimate the power of God to work in someone's life.

God is in the business of changing hearts. Think of some Bible characters who underwent significant change. What valuable truths can we absorb from them?

_____

_____

_____

_____

If change is inevitable, why is it so difficult? Which character in the film goes through the most change? Which one doesn't change at all? What are some takeaways we can learn from either character?

_____

_____

_____

LESSON 50

Entering a Child's World Expands Your World

Daddy, won't you fix my flower?
—Zuzu to her father, George

Amid George's Christmas Eve meltdown, the oddest things bring him back to his senses, if only temporarily: his daughter Zuzu and her flower. By the time he goes upstairs to see his little daughter, he has badmouthed everything from Christmas to families: Janie's piano playing, Pete's revelation that the Browns next door have a new car, their "drafty old barn" of a house, and the rigors of spelling *frankincense*.

Then there's little Zuzu, sick in bed with a cold and yet more concerned about the health of a flower she won at school. Let's face it: George is in no mood to spend a nanosecond helping fix a flower; in his mind, he's got an entire life—a pathetic, humdrum, headed-for-jail life—to fix. And yet he puts aside his chair-kicking pity party and turns his full attention to Zuzu and her flower. He pretends to repair the flower but, instead, slips the fallen-off "petals" into his watch pocket. He then places it in a glass of water next to her bed, appeasing the little girl.

It's as if Zuzu grounds him to what really matters. Here's a little girl who's more concerned about a flower than, as George has shouted at Uncle Billy an hour ago, "bankruptcy and scandal, and prison!" Children's needs—even if we might see them as trivial compared to ours—give us a gentle shaking and quiet whisper: *It's not about you, pal. Your daughter has a busted flower. Deal with it.*

That George does. His taking her concerns seriously and using a little imagination to fix the problem suggests that, beneath his anger, he's still the George we know and love. Even if it took a child to remind us.

One of the movie's crescendos comes during the scene on the snowy bridge, when George digs into his watch pocket and shouts to Bert, "Zuzu's petals!" The petals are symbols of the seemingly insignificant stuff of life that's actually so significant.

We're betting that after the Christmas Eve crowd left, when George and Mary headed for bed, he took those petals and, instead of throwing them out, tucked them somewhere as a reminder. Not only of the little daughter he loves but of what, in the swirl of adult complexity, really matters in life.

Amid the stresses of your daily routine, who brings you back to reality and reminds you of what really matters? Jot down their names and say a brief prayer thanking God for their presence in your life.

_____

_____

_____

_____

The Christmas season is the perfect time to celebrate the innocence and unbridled joy of children. As an adult, what are some ways you can return to those foundational emotions and see things from a different perspective?

_____

_____

_____

LESSON 51

It Takes Time for Some Flowers to Bloom

So mincing as to border on baby talk.
—A REVIEW IN THE *NEW YORKER* WHEN
THE MOVIE FIRST CAME OUT[1]

Some people assume that *It's a Wonderful Life* was a hit from the beginning. Not so. The movie released in December 1946 with great expectations. *Life* magazine gave it a six-page spread. *Newsweek* put it on its cover. It was rushed into theaters before year's end because it was thought that would increase its chances for winning an Academy Award come spring 1947. It did not win any Oscars. Its box-office returns were soft. And though it did win some five-star reviews, many publications scorned it.

"So mincing as to border on baby talk," wrote the *New Yorker*.[2] "Henry Travers, God help him, has the job of portraying Mr. Stewart's guardian angel. It must have taken a lot out of him."

Wrote a *New Republic* reviewer: "Hollywood's Horatio Alger fights with more cinematic know-how and zeal than any other director to convince movie audiences that American life is exactly like the *Saturday Evening Post* covers of Norman Rockwell."[3]

"For all its characteristic humors, Mr. Capra's *Wonderful Life* . . . is a figment of simple Pollyanna platitudes," wrote the *New York Times*.

Ouch.

Reviewers seemed to either love it or loathe it. Business dropped off sharply after the holidays. RKO Pictures lost $525,000 on the film. In the 1946–47 season, it ranked only twenty-seventh among the hundreds of films released. The company that produced it fell into financial ruin and ultimately liquidation. "The film itself," wrote John McDonough for the *Wall Street Journal* in 1984, "became an orphan, and passed from one corporate foster parent to another. . . . They all ignored it."[4]

And yet it is now considered by many to be the best Christmas movie of all time. The movie is on nearly every top-movie list ever compiled, eleventh on the much-respected American Film Institute's Top 100 American Films of the 20th Century.[5]

Although it was rarely watched in the 1950s and 1960s, it

rebounded in the mid-1970s. Why? Because no one remembered to renew its copyright. It went into public domain, its exclusive commercial worth irretrievably lost.

And what did that do? It infused the movie with new life. Suddenly, any television station that wanted to show the movie could do so without charge. And that's exactly what they did. It was as if a guardian angel—television—breathed life back into a movie that, like George Bailey, had lost a sense of self-worth.

Now it's undeniably among the most beloved movies ever. In September 2011, its title triggered 34.6 million hits on Google. Its online fan clubs are still going strong—seven decades after the movie came out to so many bad reviews and low box-office returns.

The lesson, of course, is that, like movies, sometimes people take time to fully blossom, to reach their potential, to "find themselves." The apostle Paul comes to mind. So does John Newton, who wrote "Amazing Grace." He was a slave trader until, at age twenty-three, he realized his wretchedness and converted to Christ.

How we begin in life isn't necessarily how we must end. Sometimes it just takes time for a particular flower to bloom.

It Takes Time for Some Flowers to Bloom

Although *It's a Wonderful Life* was a box-office disappointment in 1946, it is now considered one of the best Christmas movies ever made. What does this tell us about growth and God's timing?

_____

_____

_____

_____

God specializes in growing us over the long term. List some ways that He has changed you over time, and breathe a brief prayer of gratitude over each one.

_____

_____

_____

LESSON 52

Life Revisions Strengthen the Script

Our father, who art in heaven . . .
—Uncle Billy, in the climactic final scene,
based on how Capra originally wrote it

Nobody writes a screenplay and expects to see it on the screen just as it was originally written. It undergoes edit after edit until the final script is ready. Likewise, our own life stories can benefit from revisions too. From daring to broaden our perspectives. Daring to think bigger. Daring to risk.

In Capra's original ending, Potter appears briefly at the movie's end. After the people bring their money to George—and, of course, Principal Partridge gives the pocket watch to little Zuzu—Uncle Billy *"sinks down on his knees and starts audibly to say the Lord's prayer,"* says the script. *"Gradually, the whole roomful takes up the prayer. Even (bank examiner) Carter and the D.A. man."* A celebration follows. Janie plays the piano. Punch and wine are served.[1]

Then: "EXT. GEORGE'S HOUSE—CLOSE SHOT—AT THE DOOR. *It is still snowing. Potter, muffled in a heavy overcoat, is standing at the door. He looks at an envelope in his hand. It is Uncle Billy's money. From inside comes the Christmas carol. Potter is about to knock, but he can't. Something tells him he is unworthy to be with those inside. He sits on step*[,] *fingering money—a lonely, beaten man."*

I wouldn't think of changing the feel-good ending to *It's a Wonderful Life* as it ultimately was filmed; to do so would be sacrilegious, the equivalent of, say, reconstructing the Statue of Liberty so she's flashing a peace symbol instead of holding the light of liberty. Just wrong. That said, I like how Capra's original ending at least flirts with the idea of redemption for Potter—and I fantasize about what an alternative ending might look like.

Capra was hinting that even the most hard-crusted among us has a conscience, Potter included. Hinting that anyone, even the mean-spirited miser of Bedford Falls, might change. And at its core, isn't that what faith is all about—or should be? The idea that nobody is beyond the reach of God's endless love?

In Capra's original ending, Potter believes himself unworthy to be with the others because he sees himself as flawed beyond repair. The fact is that everybody in that living room is unworthy and flawed, hero George among them. In such an ending, what separates

George Bailey from Henry F. Potter isn't the former's perfection and the latter's imperfection. No, it's that, when standing on the doorstep of grace, George chooses to knock, but Henry does not. That George overcomes his pride (after struggling, he lets go of his, giving in to Clarence's offer of help), while Potter succumbs to self-pity (after approaching the door, stymied by his own guilt, he can't bring himself to knock).

It's fun to root against bad guys. And I confess, I laughed at *Saturday Night Live*'s "lost ending," in which George and his angry mob of friends exact revenge by pummeling Potter as if they were in a pro-wrestling ring.[2]

But unless I misunderstand Romans 3:23—"All have sinned and fall short of the glory of God"—don't we all have a little of Potter in us? And if God is gracious enough to redeem us, shouldn't we be eager for Him to redeem others?

In analyzing the movie, some have opined that Potter should have to pay the consequences for his taking the money; no argument here. But what if we were less concerned about Potter's consequences than about his heart and his soul? ("If he has one," I hear Peter Bailey rasping from his grave.) In such a case, our alternative ending might be a hybrid of the one in Capra's original script, the one actually used in the film, and the one spun in my spiritually idealistic imagination.

Potter comes to the porch, clutching an envelope, and knocks. The door opens. There stands George Bailey, the man whose family has been beaten down by Potter for decades, who nearly took his own life because of Potter having stolen the eight thousand dollars, and who might be justified in slamming the door in the man's face.

Instead, a smile slowly warms George's face. "Why, Merry Christmas, Mr. Potter," he says. "Come inside before you freeze to death. Here, let me help you with your wheelchair. Some punch? Wine?"

For a man whose cold heart might well be rooted in nobody having shown him even a sliver of such grace, it might be the catalyst for a changed life, à la Scrooge.

I know, I know. You can argue that the *It's a Wonderful Life* ending is schmaltzy enough as it is. For Potter to be wheeled into the living room by George, confess to taking the money, beg the Baileys' forgiveness, place the stolen cash in the wicker basket, hold his arms out to be handcuffed by the sheriff, and then join the chorus of "Hark! The Herald Angels Sing" with the others would be a bit much, wouldn't it?

Okay, I'd settle for the ending Capra actually used, only with a final shot from outside Potter's office of the despondent man inside, alone on Christmas Eve. Gradually the camera pans skyward to two heavenly stars that pulsate when their voices speak. "Hello, Joseph," says one. "Trouble?"

"Yes, looks like we'll have to send someone down. A lot of people are asking for help for a man named Henry F. Potter . . ."

The author writes that "our own life stories can benefit from revisions too." What parts of your own story would you like to revise and why? Which sections would remain exactly the same?

_____

_____

_____

_____

Director Frank Capra's original script offered a tiny glimpse at Mr. Potter's possible redemption. Who are some of the Bible's "bad guys" that found redemption? What can they teach us about our own lives?

_____

_____

_____

Acknowledgments

The following earned their wings with me:

—Michael Willian, whose book *The Essential It's a Wonderful Life* plumbs the nuances of the movie like no other

—Jeanine Basinger, whose *The "It's a Wonderful Life" Book* delves so deeply into Frank Capra, Jimmy Stewart, Donna Reed, and the others

—Ann Petersen, Deena Welch, Marolyn Tarrant, and Sally Welch, who read first drafts choppier than the river George and Clarence plunged into

—Dean and Lou Rea, who copyedited the final manuscript, in only a weekend

—My agent, Greg Johnson, who keeps believing in me

—Thomas Nelson Publishers, who saw potential in my "sentimental hogwash"

Acknowledgments

—Kristen Parrish and Heather Skelton of Thomas Nelson, who were insightful, encouraging, and fun to work with
—My Beachside Writers Workshop students, who politely nagged me for years to do "the *Wonderful Life* book"

Thank you all.

Notes

Lesson 1: God Honors Our "Childlike Faith"

1. Oswald Chambers, *My Utmost for His Highest*, Deluxe Christian Classics ed. (Uhrichsville, OH: Barbour, 2000 repr.), 62.

Lesson 2: Underdogs Matter

1. Michael Willian, *The Essential It's a Wonderful Life: A Scene-by-Scene Guide to the Classic Film*, 2nd ed. (Chicago: Chicago Review Press, 2006), 55.

Lesson 3: Sometimes You Just Gotta Dance

1. From "Along Comes Mary," written by Tandyn Almer and recorded by the Association in 1956 on their album *And Then . . . Along Comes the Association*. Lyrics copyrighted by Universal Music Publishing Group.

Lesson 5: Self-Pity Skews Our Vision

1. Oswald Chambers, *My Utmost for His Highest*, Deluxe Christian Classics ed. (Uhrichsville, OH: Barbour, 2000 repr.), 98.

Lesson 6: Life's Greatest Adventures Are About People, Not Places or Things

1. Oswald Chambers, *My Utmost for His Highest*, Deluxe Christian Classics ed. (Uhrichsville, OH: Barbour, 2000 repr.), 119.

Lesson 9: Stop to Count Your Blessings

1. Frank Capra, *The Name Above the Title* (New York: The MacMillan Company, 1971), xi.

2. Michael Willian, *The Essential It's a Wonderful Life: A Scene-by-Scene Guide to the Classic Film*, 2nd ed. (Chicago: Chicago Review Press, 2006), 64.

Lesson 12: Find Your Own Bedford Falls, Wherever You Live

1. Gary Kamiya, "All hail Pottersville!" Salon.com, December 22, 2001, http://www.salon.com/2001/12/22/pottersville/.

Lesson 21: Life Is Not a Bed of Roses

1. Ellen Goodman, "What's So Wonderful About It?", New York *Daily News*, December 24, 1996, https://www.nydailynews.com/bs-xpm -1996-12-24-1996359028-story.html.

2. Amy Grant, "We Believe in God," from the album *Songs from the Loft*, 1993.

Lesson 29: Look for the Best in People

1. *It's a Wonderful Life*, directed by Frank Capra, written by Frances Goodrich, Albert Hackett, Frank Capra, and Jo Swerling, film script, https://imsdb.com/scripts/It's-a-Wonderful-Life.html.

2. *It's a Wonderful Life*, film script.

3. *It's a Wonderful Life*, film script.

Lesson 30: Vengeance Is Not Ours, Saith the Lord

1. Michael Willian, *The Essential It's a Wonderful Life: A Scene-by-Scene Guide to the Classic Film*, 2nd ed. (Chicago: Chicago Review Press, 2006), 113.

Lesson 34: Fame Doesn't Equal Success, Nor Obscurity Failure

1. Oswald Chambers, *My Utmost for His Highest*, Deluxe Christian Classics ed. (Uhrichsville, OH: Barbour, 2000 repr.), entry for June 15.
2. Chambers, *My Utmost*.
3. Chambers, *My Utmost*, entry for October 1.
4. Richard Speight, Jr. (actor), interview by Jennifer Moreno, August 7, 2007.

Lesson 35: Bitterness Backfires on the One Who's Bitter

1. Jeanine Basinger, *The It's a Wonderful Life Book*, (MacMillan, 1986), 345.

Lesson 41: Helping Others Requires Sacrifice

1. Peggy Whitley, "1980–1989." *American Cultural History*, Lone Star College, Kingwood Library online, http://kclibrary.lonestar.edu/decade80.html.

Lesson 43: Desperation Can Be a Catalyst for Great Things

1. James Albert Michener, *Chesapeake: A Novel* (New York: Random House, 1974), 513–14.

Lesson 46: The Richest People in Town Might Have Little Money

1. Roger Rosenblatt, "Sometimes It's a Wonderful Life," *Time*, December 11, 2000, http://content.time.com/time/subscriber/article/0,33009,998729,00.html.

2. Rosenblatt, "Sometimes It's a Wonderful Life."

Lesson 47: The World Needs More Sentimental Hogwash

1. Paul Greenberg, "It's Still a Wonderful Life," *Journal-News* (Butler, County, OH), May 5, 2012, https://www.journal-news.com/lifestyles/philosophy/paul-greenberg-still-wonderful-life/nXw8kjKJ7O1M3lMSUT0GPN/.

2. Greenberg, "It's Still a Wonderful Life."

3. Greenberg, "It's Still a Wonderful Life."

Lesson 51: It Takes Time for Some Flowers to Bloom

1. Ellen Goodman, "What's So Wonderful About It?", New York *Daily News*, December 24, 1996, https://www.nydailynews.com/bs-xpm-1996-12-24-1996359028-story.html.

2. Goodman, "What's So Wonderful About It?"

3. Manny Farber, "Mugging Main Street," *New Republic*, January 6, 1947, accessed https://newrepublic.com/article/98662/mugging-main-street-review-its-a-wonderful-life.

4. John McDonough, "Capra's 'Wonderful Life': Color It the Holiday Classic," *Chicago Tribune*, November 24, 1985, https://www.chicagotribune.com/news/ct-xpm-1985-11-24-8503210402-story.html.

5. "AFI's 100 Years . . . 100 Movies," American Film Institute, https://www.afi.com/afis-100-years-100-movies/.

Lesson 52: Life Revisions Strengthen the Script

1. Jeanine Basinger, "Frank Capra at Work: The Original Opening Sequence," *The It's a Wonderful Life Book*, (Macmillan, 1986), 325–345.
2. You can view this humorous clip on NBC's website: https://www.nbc.com/saturday-night-live/video/its-a-wonderful-life-the-lost-ending/2723179.

About the Author

Bob Welch is the author of twenty books. In nearly four decades in the newspaper business, he twice won the National Society of Newspaper Columnists' best-column award. He does inspirational speaking across the country. Welch has served as an adjunct professor of journalism at the University of Oregon and is the founder and director of the Beachside Writers Workshop. He and his wife, Sally, live in Eugene, Oregon.